15 days
of prayer with
SAINT VINCENT DE PAUL

15 days
of prayer/series

On a journey, it's good to have a guide. Even great saints took spiritual directors or confessors with them on their itineraries toward sanctity. Now you can be guided by the most influential spiritual figures of all time. The 15 Days of Prayer series introduces their deepest and most personal thoughts.

This popular series is perfect if you are looking for a gift, or if you want to be introduced to a particular guide and his or her spirituality. Each volume contains:

- ❧ A brief biography of the saint or spiritual leader
- ❧ A guide to creating a format for prayer or retreat
- ❧ Fifteen meditation sessions with focus points and reflection guides

15 days
of prayer with
SAINT VINCENT DE PAUL

JEAN-PIERRE RENOUARD, C.M.

TRANSLATED AND EDITED BY
JOHN E. RYBOLT, C.M.

NEW CITY PRESS
Hyde Park, NY

Our thanks go to Fr. André Grinneiser and to Sister Yvonne-Marie Dubory, friendly readers of these pages. They also owe a great deal to many seminarians to whom we have had the pleasure of handing on Vincentian spirituality.

Published in the United States by New City Press
202 Comforter Blvd., Hyde Park, NY 12538
www.newcitypress.com
©2010 New City Press (English translation)

Cover design by Durva Correia

Excerpts from *Correspondence, Conferences, Documents*, vols. 1 to 12, newly translated, edited, and annotated from the 1923 edition of Pierre Coste, C.M. (Brooklyn and Hyde Park, NY: New City Press 1985–2010) are used with permission (© National Conference of Visitors, USA).

Library of Congress Cataloging-in-Publication Data:

Renouard, Jean-Pierre.
  [Prier 15 jours avec Saint Vincent de Paul. English]
  15 days of prayer with Saint Vincent de Paul / Jean-Pierre Renouard ; translated and edited by John E. Rybolt.
     p. cm.
  Includes bibliographical references (p.   ).
  ISBN 978-1-56548-357-6 (pbk. : alk. paper) 1. Vincent de Paul, Saint, 1581-1660—Meditations. 2. Spiritual life—Catholic Church. I. Title. II. Title: Fifteen days of prayer with Saint Vincent de Paul.
  BX4700.V6R4613 2010
  242'.802—dc22   2010008952

Printed in the United States of America

Contents

How to Use
This Book

*A*n old Chinese proverb, or at least what I am able to recall of what is supposed to be an old Chinese proverb, goes something like this: "Even a journey of a thousand miles begins with a single step." When you think about it, the truth of the proverb is obvious. It is impossible to begin any project, let alone a journey, without taking the first step. I think it might also be true, although I cannot recall if another Chinese proverb says it, "that the first step is often the hardest." Or, as someone else once observed, "the distance between a thought and the corresponding action needed to implement the idea takes the most energy." I don't know who shared that perception with me but I am certain it was not an old Chinese master!

With this ancient proverbial wisdom, and the not-so-ancient wisdom of an unknown contemporary sage still fresh, we move from proverbs to presumptions. How do these relate to the task before us?

I am presuming that if you are reading this introduction it is because you are contemplating a journey. My presumption is that you are preparing for a spiritual journey and that you have taken at least some of the first steps necessary to prepare for this journey. I also presume, and please excuse me if I am making too many presumptions, that in your preparation for the spiritual journey you have determined that you need a guide. From deep within the recesses of your deepest self, there was something that called you to consider Saint Vincent de Paul as a potential companion. If my presumptions are correct, may I congratulate you on this decision? I think you have made a wise choice, a choice that can be confirmed by yet another source of wisdom, the wisdom that comes from practical experience.

Even an informal poll of experienced travelers will reveal a common opinion; it is very difficult to travel alone. Some might observe that it is even foolish. Still others may be even stronger in their opinion and go so far as to insist that it is necessary to have a guide, especially when you are traveling into uncharted waters and into territory that you have not yet experienced. I am of the personal opinion that a traveling companion is welcome under all circumstances. The thought of traveling alone, to some exciting destination without someone to share the journey with does not capture my imagination or channel my enthusiasm. However, with that being noted, what is simply a matter of preference on the normal journey becomes a matter of necessity when a person embarks on a spiritual journey.

The spiritual journey, which can be the most challenging of all journeys, is experienced best with a guide, a companion, or at the very least, a friend in whom you have placed your trust. This observation is not a preference or an opinion but rather an established spiritual necessity. All of the great saints with whom I am familiar had a spiritual director or a confessor who journeyed with them. Admittedly, at times the saints might well have traveled far beyond the experience of their guide and companion but more often than not they would return to their director and reflect on their experience. Understood in this sense, the director and companion provided a valuable contribution and necessary resource. When I was learning how to pray (a necessity for anyone who desires to be a full-time and public "religious person"), the community of men that I belong to gave me a great gift. Between my second and third year in college, I was given a one-year sabbatical, with all expenses paid and all of my personal needs met. This period of time was called novitiate. I was officially designated as a novice, a beginner in the spiritual journey, and I was assigned a "master," a person who was willing to lead me. In addition to the master, I was provided with every imaginable book and any other resource that I could possibly need. Even with all that I was provided, I did not learn how to pray because of the books and the unlimited resources, rather it was the master, the companion who was the key to the experience.

One day, after about three months of reading, of quiet and solitude, and of practicing all of the methods and descriptions of prayer that were available to me, the master called. "Put away the books, forget the method, and just listen." We went into a room, became quiet, and tried to recall the presence of God, and then, the master simply prayed out loud and permitted me to listen to his prayer. As he prayed, he revealed his hopes, his dreams, his struggles, his successes, and most of all, his relationship with God. I discovered as I listened that his prayer was deeply intimate but most of all it was self-revealing. As I learned about him, I was led through his life experience to the place where God dwells. At that moment I was able to understand a little bit about what I was supposed to do if I really wanted to pray.

The dynamic of what happened when the master called, invited me to listen, and then revealed his innermost self to me as he communicated with God in prayer, was important. It wasn't so much that the master was trying to reveal to me what needed to be said; he was not inviting me to pray with the same words that he used, but rather that he was trying to bring me to that place within myself where prayer becomes possible. That place, a place of intimacy and of self-awareness, was a necessary stop on the journey and it was a place that I needed to be led to. I could not have easily discovered it on my own.

The purpose of the volume that you hold in your hand is to lead you, over a period of fifteen days or, maybe more realistically, fifteen prayer periods, to a place where prayer is possible. If you already have a regular experience and practice of prayer, perhaps this volume can help lead you to a deeper place, a more intimate relationship with the Lord.

It is important to note that the purpose of this book is not to lead you to a better relationship with Saint Vincent de Paul, your spiritual companion. Although your companion will invite you to share some of his deepest and most intimate thoughts, your companion is doing so only to bring you to that place where God dwells. After all, the true measurement of all companions for the journey is that they bring you to the place where you need to be, and then they step back, out of the picture. A guide who brings you to the desired destination and then sticks around is a very unwelcome guest!

Many times I have found myself attracted to a particular idea or method for accomplishing a task, only to discover that what seemed to be inviting and helpful possessed too many details. All of my energy went to the mastery of the details and I soon lost my enthusiasm. In each instance, the book that seemed so promising ended up on my bookshelf, gathering dust. I can assure you, it is not our intention that this book end up in your bookcase, filled with promise, but unable to deliver.

There are three simple rules that need to be followed in order to use this book with a measure of satisfaction.

Place: It is important that you choose a place for reading that provides the necessary atmosphere for reflection and that does not allow for too many distractions. Whatever place you choose needs to be comfortable, have the necessary lighting, and, finally, have a sense of "welcoming" about it. You need to be able to look forward to the experience of the journey. Don't travel steerage if you know you will be more comfortable in first class and if the choice is realistic for you. On the other hand, if first class is a distraction and you feel more comfortable and more yourself in steerage, then it is in steerage that you belong.

My favorite place is an overstuffed and comfortable chair in my bedroom. There is a light over my shoulder, and the chair reclines if I feel a need to recline. Once in a while, I get lucky and the sun comes through my window and bathes the entire room in light. I have other options and other places that are available to me but this is the place that I prefer.

Time: Choose a time during the day when you are most alert and when you are most receptive to reflection, meditation, and prayer. The time that you choose is an essential component. If you are a morning person, for example, you should choose a time that is in the morning. If you are more alert in the afternoon, choose an afternoon time slot; and if evening is your preference, then by all means choose the evening. Try to avoid "peak" periods in your daily routine when you know that you might be disturbed. The time that you choose needs to be your time and needs to work for you.

It is also important that you choose how much time you will spend with your companion each day. For some it will be possible to set aside enough time in order to read and reflect on all the material that is offered for a given day. For others, it might not be possible to devote one time to the suggested material for the day, so the prayer period may need to be extended for two, three, or even more sessions. It is not important how long it takes you; it is only important that it works for you and that you remain committed to that which is possible.

For myself I have found that fifteen minutes in the early morning, while I am still in my robe and pajamas and before my morning coffee, and even before I prepare myself for the day, is the best time. No one expects to see me or to interact with me because I have not yet "announced" the fact that I am awake or even on the move. However, once someone hears me in the bathroom, then my window of opportunity is gone. It is therefore important to me that I use the time that I have identified when it is available to me.

Freedom: It may seem strange to suggest that freedom is the third necessary ingredient, but I have discovered that it is most important. By freedom I understand a certain "stance toward life," a "permission to be myself and to be gentle and understanding of who I am." I am constantly amazed at how the human person so easily sets himself or herself up for disappointment and perceived failure. We so easily make judgments about ourselves and our actions and our choices, and very often those judgments are negative, and not at all helpful.

For instance, what does it really matter if I have chosen a place and a time, and I have missed both the place and the time for three days in a row? What does it matter if I have chosen, in that twilight time before I am completely awake and still a little sleepy, to roll over and to sleep for fifteen minutes more? Does it mean that I am not serious about the journey, that I really don't want to pray, that I am just fooling myself when I say that my prayer time is important to me? Perhaps, but I prefer to believe that it simply means that I am tired and I just wanted a little more sleep. It doesn't mean anything more than that. However, if I make it mean more than that, then I can become discouraged, frustrated, and put myself into a state where I might more easily give up. "What's the use? I might as well forget all about it."

The same sense of freedom applies to the reading and the praying of this text. If I do not find the introduction to each day helpful, I don't need to read it. If I find the questions for reflection at the end of the appointed day repetitive, then I should choose to close the book and go my own way. Even if I discover that the reflection offered for the day is not the one that I prefer and that the one for the next day seems more inviting, then by all means, go on to the one for the next day.

That's it! If you apply these simple rules to your journey you should receive the maximum benefit and you will soon find yourself at your destination. But be prepared to be surprised. If you have never been on a spiritual journey you should know that the "travel brochures" and the other descriptions that you might have heard are nothing compared to the real thing. There is so much more than you can imagine.

A final prayer of blessing suggests itself:

Lord, catch me off guard today.
Surprise me with some moment of
    beauty or pain
So that at least for the moment
I may be startled into seeing that you
    are here in all your splendor,
Always and everywhere,
Barely hidden,
Beneath,
Beyond,
Within this life I breathe.

Frederick Buechner

Rev. Thomas M. Santa, CSsR
Liguori, Missouri

References

*T*he references to the writings of Vincent de Paul used here refer to the number of the letter (L), the number of the conference to the Congregation of the Mission (C-CM) or to the Daughters of Charity (C-DC), or the number of the Document (D), in the English version of *Saint Vincent de Paul, correspondance, entretiens, documents,* edited and annotated by Pierre Coste, 14 vols., Paris, 1920–1925.

"A" (for "Abelly") refers to the first biography of Vincent de Paul, published in three volumes, 1664. The references are to the volume, book and chapter of the English translation.

"C" (for "Collet") refers to the second major biography: *La Vie de saint Vincent de Paul*, 2 vols., Nancy, 1748. There is no complete English translation.

Citations from "LdM" (for Louise de Marillac) are taken from *Spiritual Writings of Louise de Marillac, Correspondence and Thoughts,* ed., trans., Louise Sullivan (Brooklyn, NY: New City Press, 1990), with their number. [The date has been omitted.]

Glimpses
of a Life

After more than three centuries, Monsieur Vincent is still with us! Not a year goes by without some book or article being published that brings a new perspective on the past, and that shines new light on a life overflowing with an amazing and productive energy. The secret of this abundance lies in his charity, "inventive unto infinity," just like God's own love. John Paul II wrote: "The saints do not simply pass away.... What is the name of this force that resists the inexorable law of 'everything passes away'? The name of this power is love."

Why should we be adding to this accumulation of books?

We intend to shine light on the soul of Vincent's spirituality. Monsieur Vincent, that giant of charity, is an authentic mystic, an authentic man of prayer. Contemplation was the vital force of his life and it explains how he acted and how he understood his responsibilities.

He was born in April 1581 in a Catholic family living at Pouy, near the city of Dax in the south of France. He was the third son of the Depauls, farmers living on a small property called Ranquines. There they raised millet and vegetables, gathered wood from the common lands that surrounded them, and raised animals, from oxen to sheep as well as the famous pigs that Vincent bragged about. "I raised pigs," he loved to say. He was baptized the day after his birth and profited from the solid formation received from his hardworking and devoted parents, Jean Depaul and Bertrande Demoras. One of his uncles was the prior of a small stop on the pilgrimage road leading to Santiago de Compostela in Spain. It is called Poymartet and is not far from the family home. Thanks to him, young Vincent's knowledge of the faith grew and he even got a taste of Latin from his uncle. His intelligence was awakening and, when others saw him as reflective and turning toward religion, they naturally thought about priesthood. With his agreement, the family sent him to board with the Franciscans in Dax, about three miles from home. He proved to be an excellent student and became a tutor for the children of Monsieur de Comet, one of his mother's relatives.

At age fifteen, Vincent finished his secondary education. He received minor orders in the collegiate church of Bidache from the new bishop of Tarbes, a friend of the Demoras family. Thanks to his father who sold a pair of oxen to finance his higher studies, he began at age fifteen and a half at the University of Toulouse. He was clever enough to continue his studies even while having a small primary school in Buzet, and he probably spent several months at the University of Zaragoza in neighboring Spain. Whatever actually happened, he gained a bachelor's degree in theology as well as the license to teach in the university. After ordination to the subdiaconate and diaconate at Tarbes, he was ordained to the priesthood at age nineteen by Bishop François de Bourdeilles of Perigueux, on 23 September 1600. We leave it to the historians to explain how and why he was able to get the bishops to ordain him so young. His spirit of adventure is surely the reason why he has escaped the rigorous control of history from 1605 to 1608, perhaps by a captivity which is as questionable as it is possible. When we find him in Paris at the beginning of 1608, he was searching for lodgings. His Gascon countrymen and his first relationships with the upper levels of society, developed in his earliest years, led him to find Pierre De Berulle, a very influential priest, well versed in spirituality. Vincent's first culture shock in Paris troubled him. By some misfortune, he was unjustly accused of theft. Then a similar test led him to appreciate the injustices that the weak often experience. This was his trial of faith. While distributing the alms of Queen Marguerite de Valois, the first wife of Henry IV, he endeavored to help a fellow priest, a theologian suffering from doubts about the faith. Vincent supported the priest, helped him, and at the end offered himself to God in his place. The Lord took him at his word and for a long period the young priest experienced a long and dark night of the soul. He came out of this with a clear perspective on his vocation: "to devote his entire life, for the love of God, to the service of the poor."

From that time on, he chose to work for the poor. He was very happy with the country parish of Clichy where Berulle had sent him. It was there that he learned to be a pastor, and he remained until 1613 when he entered the service of the Gondis, an influential family if there ever was one. Monsieur de Gondi was the Master of the galleys of France, and his scrupulous and sensitive wife ran her household with its numerous material and spiritual obligations. Vincent de Paul was named the tutor of their children. God's providence made use of this to bring him to the bedside of a dying peasant, terribly afraid to die without confessing some sin that he had hidden for years. On his deathbed he went to confession to Vincent and then shared this joyful experience of reconciliation with Madame de Gondi.

This event let them both discover the moral distress of the poor. The following day, in Folleville, Vincent exhorted the parishioners to make a general confession of their entire life. In this way he found a new way of giving a mission. This happened in January 1617, a year in which he would make other discoveries.

Six months later, still under Berulle's guidance, he became pastor of the parish of Chatillon-les-Dombes near Lyons. An earnest appeal to his parishioners brought them to help a poor family. After this, the charitable work just started, since their pastor was organizing their natural altruism into the first "Charity," or "Confraternity of Charity." This was a group of the leading women of the parish, ready to be organized for charity. Vincent was now thirty-six years old, and from this point on he held the two keys to his future priestly life: restoring human dignity and reviving the faith of the baptized. He returned from Chatillon to the Gondis and became a missioner charged with founding Charities. He also launched upper-class women on the way of service of the poor. He discovered his true vocation and learned from events what would be his spiritual journey: the foundation of the Congregation of the Mission in 1625 and the Daughters of Charity in 1633. Important persons crossed his path: Saint Francis de Sales, André Duval, a professor at the Sorbonne and his spiritual director, and especially Louise de Marillac. She was a young widow, but still very lively and sensitive. She would become his right arm, his assistant in everything that would

impact charity. From institution to institution
Vincent's charism was being refined. The saint
had become a founder.

Nothing could divert him from his kind of
charity. Reawakening the faith of the people
demands good pastors, and for this purpose,
beginning in 1632, he began to prepare men for
priesthood. At the same time, his mother house,
Saint Lazare in Paris, became his command post.
He began the "Tuesday Conferences" in 1633,
and opened the first seminaries. Continuing his
charitable work, he put in place a special work
for abandoned infants, and he came to the help
of the devastated French provinces of Lorraine,
Picardy, Champagne and the Ile de France. He
undertook work for peace but received only rejec-
tion from the prime minister, Cardinal Mazarin.
Vincent also was the chaplain general of the galleys of France. Here was a man for all seasons!

Following the death of Louis XIII, whom
he assisted on his deathbed, he was named to
the Council for Ecclesiastical Affairs, known
popularly as the Council of Conscience. His
influence over Church and State was growing
steadily. He even dared to propose weighing the
appointments of all new bishops.

Concerning the poor, the rural Charities
transplanted to Paris became the Ladies of
Charity. The mother house fed 10,000 poor
persons and helped another 15,000 in the capital. His Daughters of Charity opened primary

schools, and their work extended even to battle-fields. He bravely sent out his missioners to Italy, Ireland, Poland, North Africa and Madagascar. His ardent temperament was bringing him into contact with all sorts of misery.

From Saint Lazare he encouraged, supported, stimulated, admonished and exhorted his own men. He wrote about 30,000 letters; we have only about a tenth of them today. Twice a week he would encourage his priests and the Sisters by giving spiritual talks to each group. He left his spiritual teaching in the *Common Rules* of his Congregation, and when he fell asleep in the Lord on 27 September 1660, he bequeathed a huge work that still reverberates. In the collective unconscious, he remains "the father of the poor," and all his friends know the expression from the funeral oration given on 23 November 1660 by Bishop Henri de Maupas du Tour, bishop of Le Puy, "He nearly changed the face of the Church."

His spiritual family is still huge: 4,000 Vincentian priests and brothers, 25,000 Daughters of Charity, 260,000 women members of the International Association of Charities, successors of the Ladies of Charity; 930,000 members of the Society of St. Vincent de Paul, based on his inspiration; 200,000 participants in Vincentian Marian Youth groups, and even some 268 religious communities look to him for their charism. This constellation of foundations is a proof of Love Incarnate.

His Journey

What a paradox! The sources that introduce us to Saint Vincent's thought are few. Nevertheless, we have fourteen volumes of various writings: letters, talks, and other documents. Vincentian Father Pierre Coste worked for over twenty-five years to edit this goldmine of texts, but they still leave us hungry for more. We have eight volumes of his letters, only 3,000 out of a total of about 30,000. We find the real man in his letters: active, a real Gascon, skillful, a diplomat, serious, humorous, but deep, spiritual and resonating with his correspondents like no one else. Then there are four volumes of his talks, or conferences. In reading them, we see that he was very skillful. Since he often spoke about his own history, his experience, and his interior life, we become familiar with him as we read his writings. This expression of his inner life is authentic, since he meditated carefully and often on where God was leading him.

Anyone who would see the young boy Vincent as far from God would be mistaken. In those days, people did nothing by halves. We see his faith at the school of his parents, and we see that the world around him spoke of God. He took his baptism seriously throughout his life (Day One). Then the young man relaxed a bit, tempted by some attempts to build a career. God seized him at the right moment and we find him at the threshold of two strong interior experiences. His faith was refounded (Day Two). Then matters became clearer and he found his own way. He recognized that he was rooted in God (Day Three). The year 1617 is always regarded as the key, in two phases. First, in favor of preaching to lead the poor peasants of Picardy to the sacrament of reconciliation, he experienced comfort in an opinion that shook his priesthood. *The poor are being damned for want of knowing the things necessary for salvation, and for lack of Confession.* (L 73) For this reason, a mission was imperative. Second, during the same year, he discovered the breadth of physical poverty. At Chatillon-les-Dombes, he laid the foundations for the Charities. The future of the poor is in God alone, but they cannot still remain hungry. Consequently, his determination was revealed without fail. He lived "completely given to God and to the poor" (Day Four). He became very devoted to the Gospel, and his plan was to do everything to build up the kingdom of God in the heart of the poor and in those who wanted to help them (Day Five). Jesus lives in the heart of the Father, and in the heart of Saint Vincent there lives Jesus. Jesus is the evangelizer of the poor, who leads every Vincentian missioner into the way of evangelization (Day Six). Jesus is also the servant of the poor, who sets all those who follow him on the way of service (Day Seven). There is a double relationship between Vincent and the poor. He can no longer pass them by, and they are for him the true sacraments of Christ, and they are also "our lords and masters" (Day Eight).

His entire spiritual theology centers on the poor Jesus. Vincent's conception of the Church was completely transformed by this and he envisions the Church as the dwelling of the poor and of the Holy Spirit (Day Nine). Where did this man get his strength? Regular daily meditation, the secret of action (Day Ten).

In Vincent there was a ceaseless movement between God and the poor, and this brings us to the heart of his teaching and his spiritual life. To go to the poor is sometimes "to leave God for God" (Day Eleven). This is much more than just a formula. Rather, it is a certainty, an act of faith. His other source of revelation and inspiration is events (Day Twelve). Besides, as a priest, he contemplated Christ the priest, whose priesthood is continued "after the manner of the apostles." Vincent was a man of the sacraments and especially a pastor, careful to develop the spirituality of the baptized and of future priests, always for the sake of the poor (Day Thirteen).

He did not accept any dead-ends, and when faced with them he elegantly changed character. He improved throughout his life and moved upward toward holiness. As part of his behavior he emphasized five basic virtues for his priests and brothers and three virtues for the Daughters of Charity (Day Fourteen). These virtues are not practiced for some apostolic purpose, but rather to support "living together." On this basis, community is necessary. We live "together for the mission" (Day Fifteen).

This man of action shows himself as deeply penetrated with God and more worried about who he was than about how he looked. He was a man of ardent charity, forged by divine love. His life was a hidden furnace and we hear him warning us about this even in our sleep: *The interior life is essential; it has to be our aim; if we lack that, we lack everything.* (C-CM 198) His life is a fire that still burns today, to be spread throughout the world!

1
Baptism
Taken Seriously

Focus Point

////////////

Many of us were baptized as infants. This is obviously not a bad thing, but it deprives of us an experience that might be fruitful throughout life. What is left is to meditate on what it means that we were reborn into Christ and that we live in his love.

////////////

In order to ... tend to our own perfection, we must be clothed with the Spirit of Jesus Christ.... We must be filled and animated with this spirit of Jesus Christ. To understand this clearly, we have to know that His Spirit is poured out on all Christians who live according to the rules of Christianity; their words and actions are diffused with the Spirit of God....

But what is that spirit diffused in such a way? How is it to be understood when someone says, "The Spirit of Our Lord is in a certain person or in certain

*actions"? Is it that the Holy Spirit is diffused in them?
Yes, the Holy Spirit personally is poured out on the
righteous and dwells personally in them. When we
say that the Holy Spirit is at work in someone, it
means that this Spirit, residing in that person, gives
him or her the same inclinations and dispositions
Jesus Christ had on earth, and they cause the person
to act in the same way — I'm not saying with equal
perfection, but according to the measure of the gifts of
that Divine Spirit.* (C-CM 196)

///////////////

When Vincent meditated on his baptism,
he discovered that the Holy Spirit had
given him the very spirit of Jesus, his very
thought processes. He was fascinated by the
One who made him live with the very spirit
of his Savior. *But what is the Spirit of Our Lord?
It's a spirit of perfect charity, filled with a marvelous
esteem of the Divinity and an infinite desire to honor
it in a worthy manner, together with a knowledge of
the greatness of His Father, in order to admire and
extol them unceasingly.* (C-CM 196)

He turned fervently in prayer toward the
Triune God who dwelled in him since his baptism. *O my Savior Jesus Christ, who became holy
so that we also might become holy, and who spurned
earthly kingdoms with their wealth and glory, having
only at heart the reign of Your Father in souls, I do not
seek my own glory but I honor my Father; if You lived*

*like that, even though with another self, since You are
God in relation to Your Father, what should we not do
to imitate You, who have raised us from dust and called
us to observe Your counsels and to aspire to holiness! Ah,
Lord! Draw us after You, grant us the grace of adopting
the practice of Your example and of our Rule, which
leads us to seek the kingdom of God and His justice and
to abandon ourselves to Him for everything else; grant
that Your Father may reign in us, and reign in us yourself, causing us to reign in You by faith, hope, and love,
by humility, obedience, and union with Your Divine
Majesty.* (C-CM 198)

Because of God, perfection was a major concern of his, as well as of his Brothers and Sisters
in community. *That's aiming high; who can reach
it? To be perfect as the Eternal Father is perfect! Yet,
that's the standard.... O Sauveur! O my brothers!
How fortunate we are to be on the path to holiness! O
Savior, grant us the grace to walk straight on it without
growing lax.* (C-CM 195)

Our saint recalled being marked at his baptism with the sign of the Cross. He made it on
himself with great devotion. *If you ask me on
what this practice is based, I'll tell you, dear Sisters,
that it's in conformity with what the first Christians
practiced. They used the Sign of the Cross to offer all
their actions to God, in conformity with the advice of
Saint Paul: "Whether you eat or drink, do all in the
name of Our Lord."* (C-DC 108)

To instinct he joined popular Christian
wisdom, which gave this gesture a sacred value.

When he made the sign of the cross he was living in God, strengthening his faith and his entire being.

To the poor of the Holy Name of Jesus Hospice that he founded, he taught this basic lesson, the basis of the Christian life, as if he were giving them a compass: *After M. Vincent had said all this, he began by questioning those good people, one after the other, on the Sign of the Holy Cross, showing them how to make it, and making it himself several times to teach as much by example as by word.* (D 49)

Baptism supposes a dual movement: both impoverishment and enrichment. One has to both die and live in Christ. *So ... you must empty yourself of self in order to clothe yourself with Jesus Christ.* (C 153)

The symbolism of baptism has spiritual effects that are the principles of life: death to sin, and freedom for a new life.

This liberty leads to rebirth, and this is a gift of God. Baptism is a call from God, a vocation, and it engenders every other call. The saint explained this very concretely to the first Daughters of Charity: *A vocation is a call from God to do something. The vocation of the Apostles was a call from God to implant the faith throughout the world; the vocation of a religious is a call from God to observe the Rules of religious life; the vocation of married persons is a call from God to serve Him in establishing a family and raising children; the vocation of a Daughter of Charity is the call of God, the choice*

His Goodness has made of her, rather than of so many others who came to His mind, to serve Him in all the ministries proper to this state of life to which He allows the Sisters to devote themselves. Your vocation, then, Sisters, is of such a nature that God, from among so many thousands of millions, looked on you, you who are with the children, you who are with the convicts, you who are in the mother house, in the hospitals, in the villages, in the parishes and said, while choosing you, one from this place, another from that, "I want this soul to sanctify herself by serving me in such or such a ministry." (C-DC 32) Whoever talks about call is talking about consecration for the work that God destines us for. Vincent often exhorted his people in this way and he invites us to live with them in a state of offering: *How happy are they who give themselves unreservedly to Him to do the works that Jesus Christ did and to practice the virtues He practiced.* (L 2039)

When a pilgrim to the village called Saint Vincent de Paul, in the Landes of Gascony, enters the parish church, he or she will be amazed to find the very font where the saint of charity was baptized. Our pilgrim can exclaim as he did: *Oh, what a happiness always to please God, to do everything we've done for love of God and to please Him! So then, Messieurs, let's give ourselves to God to do, from now on, all our actions for love of Him and to please Him. By this means, it will happen that every action, no matter how small, will have great merit before His Divine Majesty.* (C-CM 117)

Reflection Questions

What does my baptism mean to me? What responsibilities does it bring about in my life? Even if I feel alienated some times, what makes me return to these roots of my existence as a child of God?

2
A Faith Remade

Focus Point

//////////////

Who has not struggled with faith? We might wish for a conversion experience like that of St. Paul, knocked to the ground but rising with an inflexible faith. Life is more nuanced, and this is why we meditate on the gift of faith.

//////////////

I knew a famous theologian, who had long defended the Catholic faith ... in his capacity of Canon Theologian of a diocese. When the late Queen Marguerite sent for him to be with her because of his learning and piety, he had to leave his ministry; since he was no longer preaching or teaching catechism, he was assailed in his idleness by a violent temptation against faith.... And what happened after all that? God finally had mercy on that poor theologian; when he fell sick, he was instantly delivered from all his temptations. The blindfold of obscurity was suddenly removed from his eyes and his mind; he began to see all the truths of faith, but with such clarity that he seemed to feel and touch them with his finger. He finally died, lovingly thanking God for allowing him to fall into those temptations, for raising him up so successfully from them, and for giving him such great, admirable dispositions regarding the Mysteries of our religion. (C-CM 20)

////////////

*A*ny member of Monsieur Vincent's spiritual family knows that this account concerns him or her directly, since we learn from his first biographer, Bishop Abelly (writing in 1664), that the person who went to the help of the theologian is really our saint, even if he spoke of himself in the third person. Vincent worked with this man and offered himself as a victim in his place. But Vincent, in turn, found himself in an anguished uncertainty. He went through a genuine night of faith, lasting six months or as long as four years. To counter this, he wrote out the Creed, put the paper in his cassock pocket over his heart, and touched it with his hand when he was experiencing some spiritual distress. He understood the price of faith. Finally, a thought came to him: go and serve the poor. He then went to the hospital of the Brothers of Charity, the brothers of St. John of God. Then, *he thought of taking a firm and unbreakable resolve to honor*

Jesus Christ and to imitate him more perfectly than ever before by committing his entire life to the service of the poor. (A 3:11:1) This commitment, almost a vow, produced an immediate effect, and the temptation soon fell away. His faith became at its root strong and even purified.

But what kind of faith was it that animated the now mature Vincent de Paul?

First of all, it was sober and realistic. For him, there were no ecstasies, no visions. He may have had one, at the death of Saint Jeanne de Chantal in 1641. He said: *A small globe of fire appeared to him; it rose from the earth and proceeded to join another globe, larger and more radiant, in the upper region of the air; then the two became one and rose higher, and entered and expanded into another globe, infinitely larger and more brilliant than the others. He was told inwardly that the first globe was the soul of our worthy Mother; the second, that of our blessed Father; and the other the Divine Essence. The soul of our worthy Mother was reunited with that of our blessed Father, and both with God, their Sovereign Principle.* (D 34)

When he gave this kind of testimony, it was for moral and intellectual honesty, but he much preferred to affirm his lack of confidence in all sorts of exaggerated religious expressions, *lofty feelings about God, an over-heated imagination.* For him, these attitudes were suspicious. It is clear that he preferred a piety with its sleeves rolled up, ready to get to work.

Out of this comes the second aspect related to his faith: it changed his work. Everything for him was infused with a dynamic faith, transforming his daily rhythms, undertakings, conversations, even the daily mail.

The visceral center of everything was events. Life sprang up active and sturdy, depending on circumstances. He spoke of the birth of his Congregation: *Oh! That's not human; it's from God. Would you call human what human understanding didn't foresee and what the human will neither sought after nor desired in any way whatsoever?* (C-CM 180) On another day, he recalled the beginnings of the Company of the Daughters of Charity: *It may be said in truth that it's God who established your Company.... Oh no, not I!* (C-DC 20)

Although he suffered long periods of spiritual darkness, he still knew that faith takes root in peace and joy. A temptation can scrape off our surface, but still it is formative of something new. It makes a person better at understanding souls and becoming an apostle of compassion and mercy. This was clear in his letters to Louise de Marillac, a person anxious by nature who had to be led to serenity. Read this exhortation to her, for example: *Relieve your mind of all that is troubling you; God will take care of it. You cannot become involved in this, without saddening (so to speak) the heart of God, because He sees that you are not honoring Him enough by holy confidence. Put your trust in Him, I beg you, and your heart's desire will be fulfilled. Once again I repeat, cast aside all those mistrustful thoughts which you sometimes allow to invade your mind. And why would your soul not be full of confidence, since you are, by His mercy, the dear daughter of Our Lord?* (L 53) Saint Vincent distilled confidence in Saint Louise letter by letter, and he succeeded in converting her into a true spiritual animator, just as he was.

Finally, his faith simply sounds well balanced. There was nothing excessive in him. He was capable of supporting the Abbé of Saint-Cyran against the evils deployed against him, as well as of vigorously denouncing the errors of the priest's Jansenism. He wrote to the dean of Senlis, tempted by the same heresy: *If you expect God to send an angel to enlighten you more fully, He will not do so. He refers you to the Church, and the Church assembled in Trent refers you to the Holy See for the subject in question, as is apparent from the last chapter of this Council. If you expect Saint Augustine himself to return to explain himself, Our Lord has told us that if we do not believe the Scriptures, we will not believe what those returned from the dead will tell us. And even if it were possible for this great saint to return, he would submit to the Sovereign Pontiff, as he did before.* (L 2242a)

He always insisted: we must begin with faith. Then he added: *Eternal truths alone can fill the heart and lead us with assurance.* (A 3:2)

He loved to repeat the act of faith made by one of his dying confreres: *I want to die as a true*

Christian.... O my God, I believe all the truths that You have revealed to Your Church; I renew all the acts of faith I have made during my life, and because, perhaps, they did not have all the requisite conditions, I renew all those of the apostles, confessors and martyrs, etc. (L 634)

Reflection Questions

I recite the Creed at Sunday Mass, but what does it mean to me in my daily life? In my own dark moments of doubt and fear, do I turn to God in prayer? If so, what do I say? What can I do to strengthen my faith?

3
Rooted in God

Focus Point

////////////

The essence of all sin is to replace God with ourselves, taking care of "Number One," in the popular expression. Instead, we should try to look deeply into ourselves and find our roots in God, who welcomed us in baptism.

////////////

Consider the very holy dispositions in which the Christian submissive to the Will of God spends his life, and the blessings attached to all that he does: he adheres only to God, and God is the one who guides him everywhere and in everything, so he can say with the Prophet, You have hold of my right hand; and have led me by your will. *[Cf. Ps 73:23–24] God holds him by the right hand, as it were; by their holding on to one another with entire submission to this divine guidance, you'll see him tomorrow, the day after, all*

week long, all year long, in a word, throughout his life,
peaceful and tranquil, zealously tending constantly
toward God and always spreading in the souls of his
neighbor the gentle, beneficent effects of the Spirit that
animates him. If you compare him with people who
follow their own inclinations, you'll see his ways of
acting reflecting a brilliant light, and always fruitful in
results: a notable progress in his person, a strength and
energy in all his words. God gives a special blessing to
all his endeavors, and bestows His graces on the plans
he undertakes for Him and the advice he gives to others.
All his actions are very edifying. (C-CM 28)

////////////

C linging to God, being attached to him like a
poor person in distress or, better, like a child
happily holding his father's hand, is the goal that
Vincent had in trying to share his fundamental
experience. He centered all on God. He made
his own the expression of Teresa of Avila: "God
alone suffices." He opened the Gospel and he
knew instinctively that a solid house is built on
rock. Faith is the springboard and he would never
stop new activities done through faith in God, so
as to correspond to his "good will," or to do "what
is pleasing to God." This is a man who hence-
forth understood the power of God and his Word.
With God and with his word, all is possible.

God is an abyss of perfections, an eternal, very
holy, very pure, very perfect, and infinitely glorious

Being, an infinite Good who encompasses all goods and is incomprehensible in himself. Now, this knowledge we have, that God is infinitely elevated above all kinds of knowledge and all created understanding, should suffice for us to make us esteem Him infinitely, to annihilate ourselves in His presence, and to cause us to speak of his Supreme Majesty with a great sentiment of reverence and submission; and in proportion as we esteem Him, we will also love Him, and this love will produce in us an insatiable desire to acknowledge His benefits and to procure true adorers for Him. (C-CM 30)

Once Saint Vincent became rooted in God, he would never waver. Doubt no longer had any hold on him. He became a rock with the Rock itself. If he had not been born in the damp and sandy Landes, people would have said that he was a man born of granite!

How did he arrive at this kind of relationship with his God?

He gives us the answer himself: *Such is my belief and such is my experience.* (L 606) One might say that between himself and God there was a relationship of friends, since he often exclaimed: *Savior of our souls … O Lord … King of our hearts … O savior of the world.* Following the example of his spiritual teacher Berulle, he always wanted to set God in the first place: *We have to work toward esteem of God and try to conceive a great — a very great — respect for Him,* (C-CM 196) to live in his presence, to often raise our thoughts to God, and not to judge matters except after raising our spirit to Him.

For Vincent, the other, the invisible, world is right by his side. God is his interior host, the master of his house, and Vincent willingly bent to Berulle's spiritual demands: to love, to adore, to imitate. He completely loved God, who is Love: *It's certain that, when charity dwells in a soul, it takes full possession of all its powers: it gives it no rest; it's a fire that's constantly active; once a person is inflamed by it, it holds him spellbound.* (C-CM 129) He wanted to follow *the two great virtues of Jesus Christ, namely, reverence toward His Father and charity toward mankind,* (L 2334) imitating him in all ways, in all his "states" of life.

Because he experienced this privileged relationship with God, he also knew his interior as it was in himself, and he clung to God as to a relative: to the Trinitarian God, Father, Son and Holy Spirit. This is where he set his anchor.

(One of the effects) of Our Lord's love is that not only God the Father loves these souls, and the Persons of the Blessed Trinity come into them, but They also remain in them. Therefore, the soul of the person who loves Our Lord is the dwelling place of Father, Son, and Holy Spirit, and the place where the Father perpetually begets His Son and the Holy Spirit constantly proceeds from the Father and the Son. (C-CM 26)

Today, Vincent recalls for us the necessity of living in perfect communion, of helping one another. This was so important that the young founder gave his companions the Holy Trinity as their patron.

He explained to the Daughters of Charity: *I think union is the image of the Blessed Trinity. The three Persons are only one same God, united by love from all eternity. We, therefore, should be only one body in several persons, united with the same end in view for the love of God.* (C-DC 14)

He chose, finally, that, *among the good works to be performed, you will always prefer the ones in which there is more of His glory and less of your own interest.* (L 3087) The missioner, like the Sister, has as his mission the explanation of the mystery of the Holy Trinity, since it is essential, and the one who knows it will adhere perfectly to God: *Grant us this grace, Lord, of touching hearts and prompting them to love You, and especially to teach the things necessary for salvation.* (C-DC 85)

Reflection Questions

Where are my inner roots? When I worship, do I bow down before an image of myself as my creator and guide? How present is God in my daily life?

4
Totally Given to God and to the Poor

Focus Point

///////////

How can we measure the authenticity of our commitment to God? Being absorbed in prayer is wonderful, but life goes on. Vincent de Paul offers one measure of this commitment, the service of the poor. Can we ignore the poor with whom we share our towns and cities?

///////////

O Sister, how consoled you will be at the hour of death for having consumed your life for the same reason for which Jesus Christ gave His — for charity, for God, for the poor! If you only knew your good fortune, Sister, you would truly be overjoyed; for, in doing what you do, you are fulfilling the law and the prophets, commanding us to love God with all our heart and our neighbor as ourselves. And what greater act of love can one make than to give oneself, wholly and entirely, in one's state of life and in one's duty, for the salvation and relief of the afflicted! Our entire perfection consists in this. (L 2734)

//////////////

Why did this priest arrive at these convictions, like a ship arriving in port? Because he had experienced the truth that we have already mentioned. He was given to the poor to better be able to give himself to God at the end of months of doubts and interior collapse. This experience, however, came from far back in his life. Saint Vincent had known evil and what troubled his soul.

For several months in Paris he was suspected of theft. He was accused publicly from the pulpit on two succeeding Sundays of having stolen from a man's purse. In Paris in 1608 he was ostracized from Gascon society, cast off like some repulsive creature. He understood within himself the weight of iniquity, since this accusation was unjust. He kept quiet, however, while he was even treated as a poor ridiculed unfortunate: *It's not up to us to give explanations; if people blame us for something we haven't done, it's not for us to defend ourselves. God wants us to leave the discernment ... to Him, Sisters. He'll know the opportune time for making known the truth.* (C-DC 34)

After readmission into their society, he still took the side of the rejected and, day after day, he became one of them. He was on the Gospel road par excellence, the road of closeness to the poor. He would later say: *We are the priests of the poor. God has chosen us for this. This is the main purpose of our vocation, and all the rest is only accessory to it.* (C II:168) And to his Daughters he said: *Tell [the bishop] that you're poor Daughters of Charity, who have given yourselves to God for the service of the poor....* (C-DC 45)

In January 1617, at Gannes and Folleville, in the Somme, he perceived spiritual distress and he realized that he was being called to reconcile souls with each other and with God. For this purpose, he found only one possible solution, giving missions.

Six months later, in August of the same year, he was pastor of Chatillon-les-Dombes, where he encountered the illness and misery of an entire family. He sent his parishioners out on the road of charity. He acted only by the force of effective love in creating the confraternities (we might call them today parish volunteers), destined eventually to contrast with an overly regularized or mere sentimental assistance offered by others.

He perceived a constant movement between two complementary poles: the corporal and the spiritual. He understood that the first thing to do was to take care of the body, to feed it, to visit the sick and to spend time with them. His advice to the first Ladies of Charity is exactly right: *When the person whose turn it is has received from the Treasurer whatever is needed on her day for the food of the poor persons, she will prepare the dinner and take it to the patients, greeting them cheerfully and kindly. She will set up the tray on the bed, place on it a napkin, a cup, a spoon, and some bread, wash the patient's hands, and then say grace. She will pour the soup into a bowl, and put the meat on a plate. She will arrange everything on the bed tray, then kindly encourage the patient to eat for the love of Jesus and His holy Mother. She will do all this as lovingly as if she were serving her own son — or rather God, who considers as done to Himself the good she does for persons who are poor. She will say some little word to him about Our Lord ...* (D 126)

He also believed in the need for a spiritual realignment, the only way to serve the poor well. He proclaimed the Word of God, listened to the story of a peasant who felt far from God, and brought him back into peace with God. He founded the Congregation of the Mission, destined to participate in the salvation of the abandoned rural poor.

Consequently, these two poles, corporal and spiritual, made Vincent a pioneer of holistic human development, long before the concept became popular. To the priests and brothers of the Mission, he hammered away: *So then, if there are any among us who think they're in the Mission to evangelize poor people but not to alleviate their sufferings, to take care of their spiritual needs but not their temporal ones, I reply that we have to help them and have them assisted in every way, by us and by others.* (C-CM 195)

And to the Sisters he suggested: *So then, I entreat you to be very devoted to persons who are poor and take great care to teach them the truths necessary for salvation. You've noted how important that is.* (C-DC 24)

One thinks inevitably of the words of Paul VI, three centuries later: "Development cannot be restricted to economic growth alone. To be authentic, it must be well rounded; it must foster the development of each man and of the whole man.... In God's plan, every man is born to seek self-fulfillment, for every human life is called to some task by God." *(Populorum progressio,* 14:15)

Vincent especially wanted the supreme value that is God to be rediscovered through faith and charity. To participate in the life of the living God is to find the dignity of being a child of God and to live in his love. To arrive at such a perception of things, a person must be "inhabited" by God. Even better should he decide to live out a certain radical commitment. He will live as a person given to God. Vincent rises into the seventh heaven when, reflecting on the offerings made by others, he suggests that we do the same: *When a good Daughter of Charity devotes her entire life to the service of God, leaves everything, no longer possesses anything in the world — father, mother, goods, possessions, and no knowledge except of God or for God — there's good reason to think that such a Sister will one day be with the blessed. But few people have this knowledge. What a lovely sight to see a soul clothed with the grace of God, surrounded by the power of God, carrying God in her heart and never losing sight of Him! If we could see that, we'd be ecstatic with admiration; we couldn't behold the beauty of that soul without being dazzled by it.* (C-DC 85)

Reflection Questions

What are my biases about persons who are poor? Am I sorry for them or merely scornful at the mismanagement of their lives? Where is God in all this?

5
Passion for the Kingdom of God

Focus Point

///////////

We pray daily "Thy kingdom come," but what are we praying for? We might be praying for the advent of a kingdom of love and peace throughout the world. The focus of this meditation is to judge our passion for helping to bring about this kingdom.

///////////

Ah, Lord! Draw us after You, grant us the grace of adopting the practice of Your example and of our Rule, which leads us to seek the kingdom of God and His justice and to abandon ourselves to Him for everything else; grant that Your Father may reign in us, and reign in us yourself, causing us to reign in You by faith, hope, and love, by humility, obedience, and union with Your Divine Majesty. By so doing, we have reason to hope that we will reign one

*day in Your glory, which has been merited for us
by Your Precious Blood. That, my dear confreres, is
what we should ask Him at meditation; and say to
ourselves all day long, beginning on waking, "What
shall I do to make God reign supreme in my heart?
What shall I also do to extend the knowledge and
love of Jesus Christ throughout the world? My good
Jesus, teach me to do this and help me to do it!"*
(C-CM 198)

///////////////

Vincent was a very passionate person,
and this gift of God gives him his true
character. He himself admitted that he had a
rough personality: *I lose my temper, I change, I
complain, I find fault.* (C-CM 202) He was a fiery
Gascon in his soul, and he had a temper! But he
had the virtues of the strong, courage, bravery,
and firmness, but also a certain fearfulness and
above all passion, called zeal in his day. He
allowed no half-measures and always wanted to
be on the ground, ready for everything, moving
up to the front lines, encouraging, sharpening,
going to war against "insensitivity," and not
supporting those who *look for the shade…. Is
that what it means to be a Missioner, to have all our
comforts?* (C-CM 125)

People have concentrated too much on his
attention to details, on his slowness and delibera-

tion. He reflected and took his time, but he never turned back once the goal had been determined and specified. He was completely taken up with this dual principle: *There are two things to be considered here, namely, not only to do good, but to do it well.* (C-CM 177)

He was active and persevering, and from this came his desire to move and animate others, along with his stubbornness in action. He was tense and even obstinate, the qualities of the passionate. One of his biographers described him thus: "a man of action." We should follow him on his mission routes, going from village to village, from church to church, from house to house. The mother house, Saint Lazare in Paris, would give some 700 missions during his lifetime, and Vincent would take part in about one hundred of them before 1632. At age seventy-two, he left to preach at suburban Sevran. Anyone who would expect to see him confined to his office at the mother house would be mistaken. He traveled the streets of the capital from Porte Saint-Denis to the royal palace with a determination that excited popular piety. He once got out of his carriage to help a poor sufferer, giving him a ride in what he nicknamed his "infamy." He sat without hesitation at the table of the Council of Conscience, where ecclesiastical affairs were decided, to exercise some public ministry. In this way he became a sort of minister of religious affairs. He urged the women of both high society and the middle classes to continue supporting the work of caring for abandoned children. He taught the members of the Tuesday Conferences, and this organization became a sort of nursery for future bishops. He sent his preferred lay brothers, Mathurin Regnard and Jean Parre, to a very dangerous mission among the miserable refugees of the war ravaged provinces of Lorraine, Picardy, Champagne, and the Ile de France. He stopped in to visit various work areas and supervised, from far or near, all his undertakings. Jean Anouilh, the author of the script for the film *Monsieur Vincent*, was not deceived about him, and placed this lovely exchange at the end of a nostalgic conversation between this giant of charity and the queen of France. They were sitting in front of a fireplace, whose fire was slowly burning itself out, just like their lives:

> —*I've been asleep! I've been so asleep. Madame, yes, Madame, I've accomplished nothing!*
> —*So, what should a person do in life, Monsieur, to accomplish something?*
> —*More, Madame! We have been terribly negligent.*

We are at the heart of the word "*magis*" (more) used by Saint Ignatius Loyola, a word known to Vincent. "What we are going to look for is to do even more the will of God, that is, to love 'more'." (*Spiritual exercises,* 23:7) In reality, Monsieur Vincent prayed in this way: *O Savior, don't allow us to abuse our vocation.* (C-CM 152)

Was he in a hurry? No, but he was full of zeal, a lover excited by prepared action, matured under the sun of meditation. We get enthusiastic just listening to him, with our eyes fixed on the coming of the Kingdom of God. He repeated this in two of his clear and forceful statements: *We must be all for God and the service of the people;* (C-CM 167) and: *Let's strive to be animated by the spirit of fervor.* (C-CM 212) His vocabulary reveals his inner self when he freely uses the word "fire" and its derivatives: flame, enflame, burn, char, consume. His heart was expansive and he wanted the heart of his missioners to be "vast and ample." In 1657, he exhorted them: *We should desire to be so disposed ... we should be ready and willing to come and go wherever God pleases, whether to the Indies or elsewhere; lastly, to devote ourselves willingly to the service of our neighbor and to extend the empire of Jesus Christ in souls.* (C-CM 167)

It is surprising that the theme of martyrdom is so developed in this authentic mystic. He spoke of the spirit of martyrdom as clearly evident for him and for his confreres: *God grant, my dear confreres, that all those who present themselves to join the Company will come with the thought of martyrdom.* (C-CM 159) He was so consumed with this thought of the total gift of self that he invented an expression that is truly his own: "the martyr of charity." He saw the Daughters of Charity killing themselves at their work, something that tradition still sees in them, and he canonized them without hesitation: *Look upon them as martyrs of Jesus Christ, since they serve their neighbor for love of Him.* (C-DC 27)

The missioners and the Sisters imitate Christ, in the expression of Louise de Marillac, *who consumed His strength and His life in the service of His neighbor.* (LdM 513) Jesus too wanted to be like a good shepherd, who *risks his life* (L 70B) and when he sent twelve of his men, one after another, to Madagascar, some of whom died on the way or when they arrived, a mission that many around him wanted to abandon, he began to pray aloud, but without angering them: *If we weren't entangled in some wretched bramble, we'd all say: "My God, send me, I give myself to You for any place on earth where my Superiors will think it suitable for me to go to announce Jesus Christ."* (C-CM 205) With him, we say again: send us, O God.

Reflection Question

Where is the passion in my life? Do I have any passion for the things of God? If so, how far do I invest my time and interest?

6
Following Christ, Evangelizer of the Poor

Focus Point

////////////

What does Jesus mean to me? For some, he is close, a friend, a companion, or a teacher. For others, he is farther away and exalted in glory, the savior, the son of God. Vincent proposes following Jesus as the evangelizer of the poor. We can meditate for a long time on what he could mean.

////////////

Now, to work for the salvation of poor country people is the main purpose of our vocation, and all the rest is only accessory to it; for we would never have worked in ministry for the ordinands and in seminaries for the clergy if we hadn't judged that this was necessary to maintain the people and preserve the fruits of missions given by good priests. In that we imitate the great conquerors, who leave garrisons in the places they capture for fear of losing what they

*have acquired with so much difficulty. Aren't we very
blessed, my dear confreres, to live authentically the
vocation of Jesus Christ? For who lives better the way
of life Jesus lived on earth than missionaries? ... How
happy will those be who, at the hour of death, can
say these beautiful words of Our Lord, "The Lord
sent me to bring the good news to the poor." You see,
brothers, that the essential aim of Our Lord was to
work for poor persons.* (C-CM 100)

///////////////

What leaps to our eyes as we read this
passage is the predominant role of
Jesus Christ as missionary. We are in the very
heart of Saint Vincent's spiritual environment,
the French School of Spirituality, centered
on Jesus. Vincent had his eyes fixed on Jesus,
like those looking at him in the synagogue at
Nazareth. Vincent's central concern is the savior, and he presents several strong images that
can help our meditation. Jesus is our strength,
our life, and our food; (see L 2900) he is the vital
center of all the virtues, *humility, meekness, for-
bearance, patience, vigilance, prudence, and charity.*
(L 3072) *He's the Rule of the Mission;* (C-CM 198)
the eternal sweetness of men and angels; (L 1243)
our father, our mother, and our all; (L 2001) *the life
of our life and the only aspiration of our hearts;*
(L 2433) *the true model and that great invisible
portrait on whom we must fashion all our actions.*
(C-CM 128) And we can conclude with these

words taken from his first biographer, Louis Abelly: *Nothing pleases me except in Jesus Christ.* (A:1:19) There can be no doubt that the imitation of Jesus is his concern at every moment, *his book and mirror* in same author's beautiful expression. (A:3:8:2)

Saint Vincent wrote to one of his confreres envious of the pastoral successes of another: *Must not a priest die of shame for claiming a reputation in the service he gives to God and for dying in his bed, when he sees Jesus Christ rewarded for his work by disgrace and the gibbet. Remember, Monsieur, we live in Jesus Christ through the death of Jesus Christ, and we must die in Jesus Christ through the life of Jesus Christ, and our life must be hidden in Jesus Christ and filled with Jesus Christ, and in order to die as Jesus Christ, we must live as Jesus Christ.* (L 197) In this, we hear a great similarity with the philosopher Blaise Pascal, Vincent's contemporary. These words do not deceive us about the sole object of their desire and their unique activity. Pascal presents it thus: "Not only do we know God only through Jesus Christ, but we know ourselves only through Jesus Christ; we know life and death only through Jesus Christ. Apart from Jesus Christ we cannot know our life or death, God or ourselves." Pascal is more philosophical, and Vincent is more spiritual, but both are meditative and plunged into the contemplation of the Crucified.

Jesus is at the center of Vincent's spirituality and of his missionary activities.

First of all, we continue the work of Jesus, who is both the principal agent and the missionary of the Father. Jesus is God's envoy. Vincent used this passage taken from Luke 4:8 eight times in the small number of texts that we have from him: "He has sent me to preach the Gospel to the poor." He is struck by Jesus the Savior, and Vincent senses himself as having received the same mission. He also wants to be a liberator. *In this vocation, we're very much in conformity with Our Lord Jesus Christ, who seems to have made His principal aim, in coming into the world, to assist poor people and to take care of them. He sent me to bring glad tidings to the poor. And if we ask Our Lord, "What did you come to do on earth?" To assist the poor. "Anything else?" To assist the poor, etc.* (C-CM 86)

We are thus resolutely missionaries following the one and only perfect Missionary. The Gospel is the essential word to be announced to the poor. *This is your principal concern.* (C-DC 75) If this is true, our response cannot be half-hearted.

First of all, this thought is made precise through the contemplation of the Gospel mysteries. Then, once we penetrate into them, we have to present them to others, but not in grand words. Vincent fled sermons with the beautiful elegant phrases so popular in his time. He announced "the little method," of preaching, since *it's the method the Son of God used to proclaim His Gospel to us.* (C-DC 134)

Beyond the mechanics that might make us smile today (presenting the nature, motives and means), Vincent proposed a presentation that was simple, concrete, familiar, and normal. Any preacher should guard against *distorting and falsifying the word of God.* (C-DC 134) Who would not appreciate the modern ring of such a recommendation?

A mission is directed to the poor, the little ones, the simple people, those thirsting for God, and not for those looking for fancy decorations on their piety. Here is Father Vincent insisting on *the great exemplar, Jesus: In this he will imitate Our Lord when He went to sit on that stone ... and began to instruct that woman by asking her for some water. "Woman, give me some water," He said to her. So, [the Brother] can ask one, then the other, "Eh bien! How are your horses getting along? How's this? How's that? How are you doing?"* (C-CM 161)

Life is the first interest of the genuine missionary. He begins from daily life, from events, from each person's real situation, from that person's needs, worries, and concrete desires. Accompanying Jesus with the Samaritan woman, we move from the concrete and visible to the hidden, from what is evident to what is desired, from what appears to what truly is.

Reflection Questions

Where and how do I see Jesus in my daily
life? Is my religion merely comfortable or is it
sharpened by contact with the poor and the
hungry of this world? How does the imitation of
Jesus affect my life?

7
With Christ, Servant of the Poor

Focus Point

////////////

As we examine our commitment to Jesus, we meditate on his life. Vincent proposes a new lens through which to see him, as servant of the poor. Can we follow him in this?

////////////

To be true Daughters of Charity you must do what the Son of God did when He was on earth. And what did He do mainly? After submitting His Will and obeying the Blessed Virgin and Saint Joseph, He worked constantly for His neighbor, visiting and healing the sick and instructing the ignorant for their salvation. How fortunate you are, Sisters, to be called to a state of life so pleasing to God! In addition, however, you must take great care not to abuse this and strive to become more perfect in this holy state of life. You, poor village girls and daughters of workmen, have the happiness of being

among the first women called to this holy ministry....
(C-DC 2) You should also have the intention, Sisters,
of becoming truly good Daughters of Charity, for it's
not enough to be Daughters of Charity in name; you
must be so genuinely. (C-DC 7)

//////////////

*J*esus is Son of God, but there is another side
to him, according to Monsieur Vincent, the
Servant. We are all called to follow Jesus in the
way of service. This is the pure and radical gift,
activated in daily life by the same movement
of the heart: to serve the poor is to serve God!
To accomplish this, all we have to do is to look
at Jesus. He is the Word of God made flesh,
a man for others, spending his time in prayer,
living in a state of permanent communication
with his Father. "The Father and I are one."
(Jn 10:30) But Jesus is also the one who serves
human beings day after day with unlimited
devotion. "Jesus went around to all the towns
and villages, teaching in their synagogues, pro-
claiming the gospel of the kingdom, and curing
every disease and illness." (Mt 9:35)

Jesus is in his work clothes, as he recalls to
his followers in Lk 12:35: "Gird your loins,"
and as he calls us servants, a word that occurs
76 times in the four Gospels. But his example is
clearest in foot washing: "And I am among you
as the one who serves." (Lk 22:27) He witnesses

to being the person who humbles himself the most completely before his closest friends and who puts off all superiority, all divine forms, in order to gird himself for service and to wash the feet of his apostles, an activity normally reserved to a servant: *What touched me the most in what was ... has been told about Our Lord, who was the natural Master of everyone and yet made himself the least of all, the disgrace and abjection of men, always taking the last place wherever he went. Perhaps, my dear confreres, you think that a man is truly humble and has really abased himself when he has taken the last place. What? Does a man humble himself when he takes the place of Our Lord? Yes, brothers, the place of Our Lord is the last place. The man who wants to be in charge can't have the spirit of Our Lord; that Divine Savior didn't come into the world to be served but rather to serve others; He practiced this magnificently, not only during the time He stayed with His parents and with the persons He was serving in order to earn His living, but even, as several holy Fathers have felt, during the time His Apostles were staying with Him, by serving them with His own hands, washing their feet, and getting them to rest from their labors.* (C-CM 101)

We should never forget that this foot washing happened on the eve of Calvary, the place of his supreme gift! Vincent well understood the full- ness of the gift of Christ *the commandment of love and charity.* (C-CM 180) *Above all, Messieurs, if we really study that beautiful portrait we have before our eyes, that admirable model of humility Our Lord Jesus*

Christ, could it ever happen that we might allow any good opinion of ourselves to enter our mind, seeing ourselves so far removed from His exceeding self-abasement? ... Let's ask God to preserve us from this blindness; ... let's ask Him for the grace always to seek lowly places. (C-CM 165) Jesus on his knees is fully God. The Most-High has become the Most-Low.

The Daughters of Charity would call themselves and sign their names as "unworthy servants of the poor," coming out of this abasement, and this practice certainly has its teaching value in Vincent's way of thinking. From the time that he began to give missions regularly, from 1618, he founded Confraternities of Charity, voluntary associations for women. Little by little, the women of the upper classes and the nobility found it difficult to carry out the hard tasks of hauling and cleaning. Quite naturally, they turned to their servants, but they refused. Louise de Marillac then dreamed of recruiting voluntary and generous women for these tasks. Then it happened that, in God's providence, the first woman arrived, a cowherd from Suresnes near Paris, Marguerite Naseau. She had taught herself to read and write and became a teacher. She was also totally and joyfully committed to the sick. *Her charity was so great that she died from sharing her bed with a poor plague-stricken girl.* (C-DC 12) It was in 1633 that Louise finally got Vincent to agree and on 29 November she brought together the first group of the Daughters of Charity, in a house near St. Nicholas du Chardonnet in Paris.

To become a servant following Christ is also a state of life. "Being in the service of" implies a total and complete engagement. One is never "out of service," but instead always alert and ready. Saints Vincent and Louise instinctively espoused this condition of service in their own lives and those of others: *May this be our password!* (C-CM 203)

Thus, in Vincent's thought the Daughter of Charity does not "do" the service of the poor; rather, she "is" the servant of Christ in the poor. *You declare that you're devoting your life to the service of your neighbor for the love of God.* (C-DC 40) For her it is a matter of the permanent state that Saint Vincent calls "the state of charity," always and everywhere. Even if she is sick or diminished by age, she still serves in her tiny way, but she is still serving!

She simply keeps for her whole life the spirit of dependence, poverty, and simplicity. In the image of Mary, she is the servant among the servants who is placed "at the disposition of His Son." Vincent addresses Mary: *It's because of your humility that God has done great things in you.* (C-DC 88)

And he rightly recommends: *If you feel that He's calling you to hope for this grace, don't harden your heart but run to the Blessed Virgin, asking her to obtain for you from her Son the grace to share in her humility,*

*which caused her to be called the servant of the Lord
when she was chosen to be His mother.* (C-DC 98)

Jesus and Mary send us out to the responsibility of service. Being servants, no matter what
kind, even useless servants, focuses on the
word "is." It moves us away from "do" at all
costs, to guide us from quantity into quality,
from activity into listening. The follower of
Vincent obeys his teacher: *That is how Our Lord
willed to adapt Himself to the poor in order to give
us the example of doing likewise.* (L 228)

Reflection Questions

How do I work to follow the Gospel injunc-
tion of serving and not being served? In serving
others, does my commitment to them extend
beyond a casual or momentary contact? Does
service ever make me fearful? If so, what do I
fear?

8
The Poor, Our Lords and Masters

Focus Point

//////////////

Pictures of Jesus are often sweet or inspiring. Poverty etched into the faces and the bodies of others is often ugly and unsettling. If we see Jesus in them, they take on another aspect. This is why we meditate on this theme.

//////////////

The Ladies wanted me to ask you, as I now do, to find out discreetly, in every canton and village through which you pass, the number of poor persons who will need to be clothed next winter, in whole or in part, so we can estimate the amount of money needed and you can get the clothing ready early. It is thought that we should buy linsey-woolsey rather than serge. It will be necessary, then, for you to write down the names of those poor people so that when the time for distribu-

tion arrives they will get the alms, and not others who can manage without them. Now, to discern this correctly, those poor people should be observed in their own homes so you can see for yourself who are the most needy and who are less so. (L 2316)

///////////////

H ere we have Father Vincent going to the core of his true greatness. He is the man of the poor. He was heard to sigh from fatigue and from love: *The poor do not know where to go or what to do. They suffer still and these increase every day — this is my burden and my sorrow.* (C I:499) And he was even more categorical before his assembled confreres when he told him: *We are the priests of the poor. God has chosen us for them. That is our main task, and all the rest is only an addition.* (C II:168)

The poor! Nowadays, this word is troubling because it is messy and expresses a sorry state of things. How can we rightly speak about persons who have a claim on both our discretion and our shame? The tough part is always meeting a poor person, since it is easier to talk about the poor than to go with them or to share in their way of life. But the Vincentian vision of the poor demands some meditation, even contemplation. Monsieur Vincent brings us from sociology to mysticism.

First of all, he has this well-known habit of gazing. This man sees reality and scrutinizes it intensely, fixing his eyes on all those he meets on the way, rural people in the countryside, wanderers in the cities and towns, peasants, travelers, day laborers, marginalized, vagabonds, and disabled. He has pity on the sick, the elderly, orphans, and the galley convicts confided to his care, the huge number of all those unfortunate enough to be imprisoned, and those stricken with hunger. Many were out of work, the worst injustice at his time.

And then there were the beggars. In Paris in 1656 the government established the so-called General Hospital to clean up the streets of the city under the guise of benevolence. Listen to Vincent as he speaks about this. *They are going to put a stop to begging in Paris and gather all the poor in places suitable for maintaining and instructing them and giving them something to do.... The King and the Parlement have strongly supported this and, without mentioning it to me, have designated our Congregation and the Daughters of Charity to serve the poor, with the approval of the Archbishop of Paris. However, we have not yet decided to commit ourselves to this work because we are still not sure that it is the Will of God. If we do undertake it, it will first be on an experimental basis.* (L 2222)

Secondly, Father Vincent was not content just with a vision of the poor. He could not erase the hard times of his infancy and youth, and he understood only too well the value of work to let the poor be deprived of it. He thus reacted strongly and settled down to addressing emergencies while giving them something to eat.

To nourish, to help out in immediate needs — this was his understandable reflex.

But he did not just stop there. He wanted everyone to pitch in whenever this was possible. The case of aid to the provinces devastated by the civil war called the Fronde is a good example of this. He gave very precise orders to Brothers Regnard and Parre, his assistants in aiding victims of violence.

He wrote to Brother Jean Parre: *A small sum of money will be set aside to help a few poor persons to sow a little patch of land — I mean, the poorest, who would be unable to do so without such assistance.... You could recommend to them in passing to prepare a small plot of land, to plough and fertilize it, and to ask God to send them some seed to plant in it. In addition, without making them any promises, give them the hope that God will provide.*

They would also like to enable all the other poor people who have no land — men as well as women — to earn their own living, by giving the men some tools for working and the girls and women spinning wheels and flax or linen for spinning — but only the poorest. (L 2936) Clearly, he is giving personal attention to the case.

He even had recourse to a system of news-letters established by Maignard de Bernieres. These were written and distributed like so many pamphlets with information about individual situations, and they were destined to touch hearts and open purses. He appointed a Superintendent of Charity among his confreres to coordinate the needs and relief efforts. But there was clearly much more for this saint of charity. For him, any poor person opens up for us the one who suffers, the one who bears the weight of the miseries of the world, none other than Jesus, poor and humbled. A poor person is the "sacrament of Christ." Vincent expresses this mysticism of the poor in words that have circled the world: *I must not judge a poor peasant man or woman by their appearance or their apparent intelligence, especially since very often they scarcely have the expression or the mind of rational persons, so crude and vulgar they are. But turn the medal, and you will see by the light of faith that the Son of God, who willed to be poor, is represented to us by these poor people.* (C-CM 19)

Our saint loved to make his own the definitive expression of the glorious Christ, judge of all: "Whatever you did for one of these least brothers of mine, you did for me." (Mt 25:40) He said to the Daughters of Charity: *Poor people are our masters; they're our kings; they must be obeyed;* (C-DC 106) they are our lords, who in some way overturn the established system, but he was speaking with such force right in the middle of the seventeenth century! The social pyramid has been upended, and the first become the last. The rich and the great ones of this world are called to serve.

Today more than ever, the dignity of the poor calls into question our own dignity. Whether we want to or not, whether we know it or not, the relationship we have with them judges our faith.

Reflection Questions

Do I believe, deep down, that persons who are poor have any dignity? What, if anything, can I learn from them? Am I open to doing so? What opportunities present themselves in my life to practice this?

9
The Church,
City of the Poor

Focus Point

////////////

Paul the Apostle taught the Church about the mystical body of Christ. We meditate on this reality, not with tender and warm emotions alone, but with an experience of life in all its difficulties. Do we believe that others can have a claim on us?

////////////

All of us make up a mystical body, but we're all members of one another. It has never been heard that a member, not even among animals, was insensitive to the suffering of another member, or that one part of a person's body may be bruised, wounded, or injured and the other parts don't feel it. That's impossible. Every part of us is in such sympathy with one another and so interconnected that the pain of one is the pain of the other. Since Christians are mem-

*bers of the same body and members of one another,
with even greater reason should they sympathize with
one another. Quoi! To be a Christian and to see our
brother suffering without weeping with him, without
being sick with him! That's to be lacking in charity;
it's being a caricature of a Christian; it's inhuman;
it's to be worse than animals.* (C-CM 207)

//////////////

Vincent has chosen the better part, and
he shares it enthusiastically with his
confreres: *So then, my dear confreres, poor persons
are our portion, the poor!* (C-CM 180) He then
enthusiastically told Daughters of Charity, *in
serving persons who are poor, we serve Jesus Christ.
How true, Sisters! You are serving Jesus Christ in
the person of the poor. And that is as true as that
we are here.* (C-DC 24) The surprising thing for
someone who reads our saint closely is Vincent's
insistence on creating structures, in weaving
new relationships precisely concerning the poor.
He was constantly starting new organizations,
and he made all their parts work together.
The Daughters of Charity, the Missioners of
his congregation, the Ladies of Charity, the
Confraternities of Charity, clergy and civil
authorities, women and men of good will were
all invited to come together to relieve the needs
of the poor. He managed to assemble in this
huge outpouring of generosity both cowherd

and queen, poor country girls and noblewomen bedecked with their jewels.

In this way he began a new way of "doing Church." He knew instinctively that God does not distinguish among human beings, and he had meditated enough on the Acts of the Apostles to remember that the earliest Church was inviting its people to this same union in the Spirit.

The People of God in communion is his prophetic vision of a Church coming to terms with the Gospel.

In his way of thinking, we are far from the silk and the gold of the prince-bishops, the commendatory abbots, and the often absent hierarchs. As a member of the Council of Conscience from 1643, he learned how to name worthy priests as pastors of vacant dioceses. He knew the decisions and the outlook of the Council of Trent. He wanted to move toward missionary effectiveness and judged that *the Church has ... too many useless [priests], and even more who tear her apart. Her great need is evangelical men who work to purge, enlighten, and unite her to her Divine Spouse.* (L 960) One day we see him clearly refusing to use his influence to have a candidate advance to the priesthood: *I would consider it a matter of conscience to do anything to have you take Holy Orders, especially priesthood, because it is a misfortune for those who enter it by the window of their own choice and not by the door of a legitimate vocation.* (L 2792) We can readily imagine the face of his correspondent, an attorney, when he received this sort of answer to his rejected pleading.

Father Vincent's care was elsewhere.

He had been a rural pastor, in Clichy, in contact with the peasants of a good parish: *I don't think the Pope himself is as happy as a Pastor in the midst of such good-hearted people.* (C-DC 55) In Chatillon, a prosperous and well-run parish, he succeeded, since the people were of good will.

In Montmirail, he converted a Protestant with an evangelical lesson. He explained this man's turnaround: *The [man] was curious enough to attend the sermons and catechism lessons; he saw the care that was taken to instruct those who did not know the truths necessary for their salvation, the charity with which the priests adapted themselves to the weakness and slowness of mind of the most unrefined, and the marvelous effects the zeal of the Missioners brought about in the heart of the greatest sinners. Moved to tears, he went to find the saint and said to him, "Now I see that the Holy Spirit is guiding the Roman Church, since such care is taken in the instruction and salvation of poor village people; I'm ready to enter it whenever it will please you to receive me."*

Here is Saint Vincent before the Church of the poor, perfectly in sync with it. When the Protestant's profession of faith was over, Vincent exclaimed in amazement: *Oh! What a happiness for our Missioners, ... to verify the guidance of the Holy Spirit on His Church by working, as we do, at the instruction and sanctification of poor persons!* (C-CM 21)

He still shows us concretely that the evangelization of the poor is a criterion for the active presence of the Holy Spirit in the Church. We might say that Vincent de Paul based all his pastoral action on this ecclesial foundation.

In this way the Mystical Body of Christ was not some theological abstraction. He devoted his life to it. He knew that the Church at its deepest reality, the great assembly of the children of God, embraced preferentially its littlest members. He rejoiced over this, since the Spirit is at work in the hearts of the poor, as it is in the hearts of all persons of good will.

It is not alien to our subject to recall Bishop Jacques Benigne Bossuet, in his time the most popular preacher in the royal chapel and the large churches in Paris. In 1659 Bossuet gave sermons on "the eminent dignity of the poor," a clear echo of the thinking of Vincent de Paul. The two knew each other, esteemed each other, and worked together. We find in the text of this sermon a dominant idea: the Church that Jesus Christ willed is, first and foremost, with all due deference to the rich and the powerful, the world of the voiceless and those without social position. How can we not meditate on this today?

"It belongs to the Savior alone and to the politics of heaven to build us a city that is the true city of the poor. This city is the Church. Christians, if you ask me why I call it the city of the poor, I will tell you the reason for this proposal of mine. At its root, the Church has been built only for the poor, who are the genuine citizens of this blessed city that the Scripture has called the City of God…. You rich, come then to this church. Its door is open at last, but it is open for you in favor of the poor, and on the condition of serving them. It is for love of these children that entry is granted to strangers. Behold the mystery of poverty. The rich were strangers, but the service of the poor makes them citizens…. You rich, beg God for his mercy." (Sermon on the "Eminent Dignity of the Poor.")

Reflection Questions

Do I ever need to temper my activism with reflection on what I am really doing in my service of others? How does my reception of the Eucharist color my relationships with others? Can others who know of my faith see the difference it makes in my life?

10
Prayer, the Soul of Action

Focus Point

///////////////

The great spiritual teachers tell us that we must draw our strength from deep wells. If we draw only from ourselves, we will go dry. If we draw from prayer, waters will flow incessantly. This is what we meditate on today.

///////////////

Something important to which you must faithfully devote yourself is to be closely united with Our Lord in meditation; that's the reservoir where you'll find the instructions you need to carry out the ministry you're going to have. When you have a doubt, turn to God and say to Him, "Lord, You who are the Father of Lights, teach me what I must do on this occasion." … You must also have recourse to meditation to ask Our Lord for the needs of those whom you'll be guiding. Rest assured that you'll produce greater results by this means than by any other. Jesus Christ, who must be your model in all your ways of acting, was not satisfied with His sermons, His works, His fasts, His blood, and even His death, but He added meditation to all that. He had no need of it for himself; it was, then, for us that He prayed so often, and to teach us to do the same, both for our personal concerns and for what concerns those whose saviors we must be, together with Him. (C-CM 153)

///////////////

*G*od, the Kingdom, the poor: how can we accomplish such a project? Vincent had only one secret, prayer. For him, this was the passion of his life, "the center of devotion." When he broached this subject, which he held dearly, he had something like a conditioned reflex, and he used images that expressed the vital elements that he wanted to employ to communicate its importance, in fact, its absolute necessity. He called prayer the soul, air, food, dew, reservoir, fountain of youth, sun, daily bread, nursery. His famous expression is very strong: *Give me a man of prayer, and he'll be able to do anything.* (C-CM 76) At the same time, he was giving spiritual direction to his young confrere, Antoine Durand, whom he appointed superior at Agde at age twenty-seven, and he urged him to love his parish, the major seminary and the band of missioners. Durand could either be presumptuous or be crushed by his responsibility. His teacher and friend encouraged him by the great means of prayer and by the principle that arose from it, namely, the imitation of Jesus Christ. There could never be one without the other.

To make mental prayer, daily, for an hour … the indications are there in his writings, and they are powerful and penetrating. They transcend time to reach us and yank us out of our bourgeois state. Vincent believed that, without prayer, there is great danger of falling into "insensibility" or even disgust about God. One day in 1648 he said to the Sisters: *Never stop praying at all, for meditation is so excellent that we can never make it too much.* (C-DC 37)

We can contemplate Vincent in a state of prayer. He prayed spontaneously, in his letters and in his talks: *O God my Lord, please be the bond of their hearts;* (L 989) *O my God, we give ourselves entirely to you;* (C-DC 3) *O my God, we give ourselves to You for the accomplishment of your plan for us;* (C-DC 15) *My Lord and my God, Jesus Christ my Savior, the most amiable and loving of all men.* (C-DC 28) His exclamatory style was the language of his heart. Against it, there could be no appeal: *The grace of vocation depends on prayer, and the grace of prayer depends on rising. If then we are faithful to this first action, if we come together before Our Lord and present ourselves all together to Him as the first Christians used to do,*

He will give Himself in turn to us, will illumine us with His lights, and will Himself accomplish in and through us the good we are bound to do in His Church. Lastly, He will grant us the grace of attaining the degree of perfection He desires of us so that we may be able one day to possess Him fully in the eternity of the ages. (L 1176)

There, in the daily heart-to-heart conversation with the Love that dwells within us, we learn to do his will: *It's in prayer that He takes total possession of hearts and souls.* (C-DC 37)

This has to move into action, what the seventeenth century called the "resolution," the principal part of the mental prayer. It deals with changing our life and behavior, our way of living and acting, even conversion. Prayer should look toward the practical, *come down to particulars,* (L 544) as Saint Francis de Sales suggested. One is to work to suppress a precise defect or acquire a virtue, point by point, element by element. A little daily step verifies and adjusts the patient's state.

It is important not to lose sight of life. Mental prayer is the engine for action, the privileged place where the direction of our existence becomes evident. And Vincent showed this in a way that still speaks through what Vincentian tradition calls the "the president's method."

In this respect, I must tell you how edified I was recently by a President, who made his retreat with us about a year ago. Speaking to me about the little examination of conscience he had made on his rule of life, he said that, by the grace of God, he thought he had failed to make his meditation only twice. "But do you know, Monsieur, how I make my meditation? I foresee what I'll have to do during the day and take my resolutions accordingly. I'll go to the Courts of Justice; I'll have to plead such and such a case; perhaps I'll meet some person of rank who may, by his advice, try to corrupt me. With the help of God's grace, I'll be very much on my guard against that. Perhaps someone will offer me a present which I'd very much like to have; I won't take it! If I feel inclined to rebuff somebody, I'll speak to him kindly and graciously."

Well, Sisters, what do you think of that sort of prayer? ... You can make your prayer in this way, which is the best way; for you shouldn't make it in order to have exalted ideas, ecstasies, and raptures — which are more harmful than useful — but only to perfect yourselves and make you truly good Daughters of Charity. So, your resolutions should be something like this, "I'm going to serve some poor persons; I'll try to go to them with a simple, cheerful attitude to comfort and edify them; I'll speak to them as if they were my lords." (C-DC 4)

Could anyone say it better? Our thoughts are suspect, but promises made and kept are exemplary. These all come from God, the Light of our hearts: *I ask You, my Savior Jesus Christ, to*

pour forth abundantly on this Company the gift of
prayer, so that, by knowing You, it may acquire Your
love. (C-DC 37)

Reflection Questions

Was there a time in my life when my prayer
was more important to me than it is today? If so,
what happened to change this? What can I do to
improve my prayer life? Is my well full or empty?

11
"To Leave God for God"

Focus Point

//////////////

Balance is a skill that we learn as children from our parents. Balance in adult life is more complex, with its competing values and expectations. We meditate on where God is to be truly found. From this comes balance.

//////////////

Now there are certain occasions on which the order of day can't be kept; for example, someone will come to your door at prayer time to ask a Sister to go to see a poor, sick person who needs her; what will she do? It will be all right for her to go and to leave her prayer — or rather to continue it, because that's what God is ordering. For you see, charity is above all Rules, and everything comes down to that. If it's a woman of rank, you have to do what she tells you. In that case it's leaving God for God. God calls you to make your prayer, and at the same time He calls you to that poor, sick person. That's called leaving God for God. (C-DC 105)

//////////////

*T*his teaching from Saint Vincent is not the only one like it. In the texts that we have in our possession, we meet it twenty times. Of course, it is often easy to say that we should as much as possible catch a spiritual meeting or a Mass, but the same teaching is always there: we should give special attention, in case of need, to the service of the poor. This is what it means to say: To leave God for God. He took this famous expression from important teachers, like Thomas Aquinas, Teresa of Avila in the "fifth mansion," Camillus de Lellis, whose hospital he could have seen during his one-year stay in Rome, Father De Berulle, and others. He knows that this is said in faithfulness to the Gospel, and he insisted on it in every circumstance.

First, concerning Mass: *For example, if the good pleasure of God were that you should go on a Sunday to nurse a sick person instead of going to Mass, even though that's a matter of obligation, you should do it. That's called leaving God for God.* (C-DC 68) And then: *As far as possible, you should hear Mass every day, but if you are needed in the house or have to attend to poor persons, you should have no qualms about omitting it.* (C-DC 6)

Next, concerning meditation, he repeated: *To nurse the sick is to make your prayer;* (C-DC 30) and once again: *It's time for prayer; if you hear poor persons calling for you, mortify yourselves and leave God for God, even though you must do your utmost not to omit your prayer, for that's what will keep you united to God; and, as long as this union continues, you'll have nothing to fear.* (C-DC 61)

Finally, he draws a major and general conclusion: *The service of the poor must be preferred to everything else.* (C-DC 21)

In short, this is a constant precept, but flexible and balanced. We understand this affirmation: *The duty of charity is above all rules* (L 2110) which he wrote to a Sister with problems in her community and in communication with her spiritual director. When she stood back from herself, he brought a personal correction to passing problems. Helping the sick is the antidote for every difficulty.

In this way there grew up an unexpected hierarchy of values. Instead of the classical points generally taught, Vincent drew up a different priority, beginning with the service of the poor, not that it was exclusive, but because it was first. This demands permanent examination, both personally and in community. Of course every consecrated person draws interior resources from prayer, the Mass, and the rule, but this service of the poor is the focal point of all his or her energies: *Charity is the queen of virtues, we must leave everything for it.* (L 2788)

These two loves are, in fact, but one. Saint Vincent was able to interiorize Mt 22:37–39: "You shall love the Lord, your God, with all your heart, with all your soul, and with all your mind. This is the greatest and the first commandment. The second is like it: You shall love your neighbor as yourself." He presented a magnificent little parable to express it: *A father who has a handsome, grown-up son is pleased to watch from a window as the boy walks boldly down the street, and this gives him unimaginable joy. In the same way, Sisters, God sees you, not through a window but everywhere, no matter where you may be, and He watches how you go off to render service to His poor members. If He sees you going about it in the right way with the sole desire of rendering Him service, it gives Him inexpressible joy. It's His great pleasure, His joy, His delight. What a happiness, dear Sisters, to be able to give joy to our Creator!* (C-DC 41)

God is served in the neighbor, or to say it better, Christ is. Our saint said: *And that is as true as that we are here.* (C-DC 24) This was his way of concretizing the absolute reality of the love of God. Relationship to Christ happens in an immediate relationship to the poor, whether we realize it or not. Vincent repeated: *All our work consists in action,* (C-CM 25) an action that is directed to Christ through the poor. Jesus is this God-of-the-poor. As the president of the Dominican committee on Justice and Peace, Alain Durand, O.P., wrote, "the presence of Christ confers on our activity for the poor a radical power of decision: our acts or their omission become capable of setting us on the way toward either life or death." That is why there is continuity between the God sought out in prayer and the poor encountered in our lives. It is always the God of Jesus Christ who shows such an avowed predilection for the poor, corresponding to the sentiment of justice that dwells in him. He wills even more the salvation of the little ones left to themselves than the salvation of everyone. If he wishes that all be saved, then for an even greater reason, he shows a privileged love for those who find themselves in an exceptional situation of inequality.

Dear reader, Father Vincent has brought you thus far. Think about your life and the weight of your years. What have you accomplished? The only universal criterion that should weigh on your soul is the one we find summarized in the Gospel: "you have done it to me." You can and should give time to God in prayer, but you should spend equally as much time and perhaps more in doing justice. And do not be one of those who cannot stand to hear the Church that you love talking about its "preferential option for the poor." Listen to the cry of your friend Vincent: *The service of poor persons ... this is your principal concern, for which you must leave everything.* (C-DC 75)

Reflection Questions

What have I done for justice today? Where is my balance between the demands of my interior life and those of my exterior life, with its many responsibilities? How do I decide? How do I regain my balance when I have stumbled?

12
Daily Life, Source of Inspiration and Action

Focus Point

//////////////

Where can I find God? Vincent's meditation led him to concentrate on the presence of God in the events of daily life, and not in ecstasies and emotions. Our meditation today is on discerning the hand of God, past, present, and future. We wonder how God's providence manifests itself.

//////////////

What have our Missioners in Barbary and Madagascar undertaken? What have they carried out? What have they accomplished? What have they suffered? A single man takes on the care of a galley where there are sometimes two hundred convicts: instructions, general confessions to the healthy and to the sick, day and night, for two weeks; and at the end of that time, he gives them a party, going himself to buy a steer and have it cooked; it's their delight; one man alone does all that! Sometimes he goes off to the farms where slaves are placed, and he goes in search of the masters to ask them to allow him to work at the instruction of their poor slaves; he takes them on their free time and helps them to know God; he gets them ready to receive the sacraments, and at the end he gives them a treat and has a little party for them.... The Missioners preach, hear confessions, and teach catechism constantly from four in the morning until ten, and from two in the afternoon until nightfall; the rest of the time is spent praying the Office and visiting the sick. Those men are workers, they're true Missioners! ... If we can do nothing of ourselves, we can everything with God. Yes, the Mission can do anything because we have in us the seeds of the omnipotence of Jesus Christ. (C-DC 125)

/////////////

*I*f we need any further indication about the quality of Father Vincent's life, it is here. God speaks to us, and He speaks to us by His Word, as well as by the events of daily life. He always reveals something that strengthens us and that is symbolic for those who wish to receive his message. Even today, those who follow Vincent are invited to live in awareness, always on the lookout for the "signs of the times," a Gospel expression used by the Second Vatican Council that puts us in a state of watching.

Saint Vincent built his spiritual path and his profound thinking on the events of life. These events mark out his life, as they do for his Congregation where, as we have just read, he shows us how to move from the ardor of certain individuals to a collective enthusiasm. When he first arrived in Paris in 1608, he was falsely accused of theft, and here he experienced injustice. This event ground him down. When he became pastor of Clichy in 1611, this event awakened his pastoral sense. In experiencing his dark night of faith around 1613, this event built him up again. When he went to the bedside of a dying man in 1617 to hear his last confession, this event moved him forward in his pastoral choices. The same thing happened in Chatillon the same year.

We see him again receiving money from the Gondis to begin his new congregation. This event fortified him in his apostolate. By chance he was talking with Bishop Potier of Beauvais as they were traveling in the bishop's carriage, and this led him to respond by helping candidates preparing for ordination. This event put him into paths that his sons would often follow. He met with a young aristocrat, Louise de Marillac, who had passed through her own painful doubts and was looking for some balance in her life. This event led to the Daughters of Charity. When one day Marguerite Naseau came to him to offer herself for the service of the poor, *moved by a powerful inspiration from heaven,* (C-DC 12) this event was like a flash of lightning and it opened the way to the first Daughters of Charity. He often repeated: *God is the one who did all this.* The same was true for the beginning of the work for abandoned children: *Oh! how indebted you are to God for having given you the inspiration and the means of meeting these great needs!* (D 198) We could still explain the other works of our saint: beggars, prisoners, galley convicts, slaves in North Africa, refugees, the sick and the mentally disturbed, victims of floods and exiles. This man was a sentinel and everything overtook him as he was watching and waiting.

His Gascon peasant origins were not the only reason why he was pragmatic and concrete. He lived an intense interior life, and his spiritual experiences led him to regard the events of daily life as the bearers of the message, and especially of the active presence, of Jesus Christ. He himself decodes these events. For the two major ones, the founding of the Congregation of the Mission and of the Daughters of Charity, he affirmed: *It was God, and not I* (C-DC 20) and we see him marveling at the wonders that God had wrought: *Who would have thought then, brothers, that God intended to do, through the Company of the Mission, the good that we see it doing, by the grace of God? Who knew that He intended to make*

use of it to go to seek out those poor Christian slaves
on the farms deep inside Barbary [in North Africa]
to withdraw them, if not from a hell, at least from a
purgatory? And who knew that He wanted to make
use of it also in so many other places, as we see Him
doing? (C-CM 112)

As long as God is at work, that is enough!

In this way we see two results: the events
of life are at one and the same time the place
of receiving divine revelation and the place of
human activity. God is always there, acting and
moving him and those he was responsible for.
Father Jean Morin wrote: "Vincent read events
and he read the Gospel, and both of them clari-
fied and nourished his faith." In *Saint Vincent de*
Paul sous l'emprise chrétienne, Louis Deplanque
remarked: "God is constantly at work. He is
present in the thousand twists and turns of the
circumstances in which Vincent found himself
caught up. God is likewise present in the flow
of life and Vincent adapted his action to His
laws." (P. 65)

For his own part, Vincent accorded great
importance to what was happening. Even if
he were blind, he would see the hand of God
and draw out the consequences. This is what
happened when he lost the case about the farm
of Orsigny. This was an important source of
income for the poor. After the death of the
donors of the farm, their heirs began a lawsuit

to recover the farm for themselves. Vincent reacted strongly in the presence of his men assembled for a conference. *O Lord, You yourself have handed down the decision; if it pleases You, it will be irrevocable; and, so as not to defer its execution, here and now we make the sacrifice of this property to Your Divine Majesty.* (C-CM 189) And later in the same conference: *Oh, if God were pleased to recompense this temporal loss by an increase of trust in His Providence, abandonment to His guidance, greater detachment from earthly things and self-renunciation,* O mon Dieu!

This appeal to Divine Providence is vintage Vincent de Paul. He knew that it was good to live according to God's rhythm, to follow in his footsteps, to seem to go slowly, so as not to "tread on the heels" of Providence, to live as available and confident. Everything else is just bubbling on the surface.

Reflection Questions

Do I rely on preparedness and good luck, or is my focus on the hand of God in my life and in the lives of others? Where do I sense God leading me in my life, long-term and short-term? What is my goal, and how will I know when I reach it?

13

A Priest
Serving Priests

Focus Point

////////////

The People of God are priests for God. The Church chooses some members to follow Jesus the priest in ordained ministry. We meditate today on Jesus the priest and his priestly commitment to the poor and marginalized.

////////////

The distinguishing mark of priests is a participation in the priesthood of the Son of God, who has given them the power to sacrifice His own Body and to give it as food, so that those who eat it will have eternal life. That's a totally divine and incomparable characteristic, a power over the Body of Jesus Christ that angels admire, and a power to forgive the sins of the people, which is a great source of amazement and gratitude to them. Is there anything greater and more admirable? Oh, Messieurs! What a great thing a good priest is! What is there that a good priest can't do and what conversions can he not obtain? … The success of Christianity depends on priests. (C-CM 4)

//////////////

*T*his passage is famous in Vincentian litera-
ture. It brings us directly into what is best
in Saint Vincent de Paul. He was a priest of Jesus
Christ and fully a priest for the poor. His priestly
journey was jumbled and chaotic, but it grew.
He moved step by step into the excellence of the
priestly vocation, such as it was understood in
the seventeenth century, when the spirit of the
Council of Trent was being awakened.

His vocation was proposed to him by his
family. An active and passionate person, he
took up the challenge, and he was called to
priesthood. From 1613 on, we can say that he
was a good priest and a zealous pastor. He had
interiorized and personalized his vocation. He
had become a man of prayer, a careful reader
of spiritual authors, an excellent preacher, an
eminent catechist, and he was surrounded by
fervent priests and laity. By then he had moved
from priesthood as an idea to priesthood as a
reality, from wishes to a firm and tenacious
commitment. He could pray: *O Lord, give us the
spirit of Your priesthood, which Your Apostles and
the first priests who followed them had; give us the
true spirit of this sacred character you bestowed on
poor fishermen, artisans, and needy people of that*

time, to whom, by Your grace, you communicated this great, divine spirit. For we, too, are only weak people, Lord, poor workers and peasants; and what comparison is there between us, wretched men, and such a holy, distinguished, heavenly ministry! (C-CM 141)

By the year 1617 he was well prepared spiritually for his mission. He knew that he owed everything to the grace of God, as his various comments showed. Concerning a relative who was looking toward priesthood, he wrote to a compatriot, Canon Saint-Martin: *As for myself, if I had known what it was when I had the temerity to enter it — as I have come to know since then — I would have preferred to till the soil than to commit myself to such a formidable state of life.* (L 2027)

These lines testify to his vivid awareness of the greatness of the priesthood. He humbled himself only to exalt the excellence of the priesthood. In this, he was reflecting his own period. In Paris, he shared the insights of the pioneers of the French School of Spirituality, grouped around Pierre de Berulle, who looked at priests as "another Christ."

Vincent had a great esteem for the sacrament of Holy Orders. *There's nothing greater than a priest, to whom Christ gives all power over His natural and His mystical Body, the power to forgive sins, etc.* (C-CM 195) The priest gives life to the Mystical Body, he teaches it, he helps to unify it, to reconcile it, and he prays with its members. The road to holiness par excellence is being identified with Christ the Priest. Everyone, both clergy and laity, are called to this. But priests do so in a specific way, when, like Jesus, they practice two great virtues: *reverence toward His Father and charity toward mankind.* (L 2334) Adoration and mission are two predominant themes in Berulle. For Vincent, the priest must celebrate the Eucharist with great respect. *It's not enough for us to celebrate Mass, but we must also offer this Sacrifice with the greatest devotion possible, in accord with God's Will, conforming ourselves, as far as is in us, with His grace, to Jesus Christ offering himself, when He was on earth, as a sacrifice to His eternal Father.* (C-CM 75) The priest builds up the Mystical Body of Christ by his pastoral work and by taking on himself the burden of his people's sorrows: *Those poor people give us their goods for that purpose; while they're working and struggling against poverty, we're like Moses and must continually raise our hands to heaven for them.* (C-CM 84)

Vincent does not separate the spirituality of the priest from the spirituality of the baptized. He loved to repeat that his Congregation was made up of both clergy and laity who were following the way common to all Christians, since its members belonged to the "Order of St. Peter." He did not distinguish between a properly priestly spirituality and a pastoral and missionary spirituality. To be a lay brother, for him, derives from the person's baptismal dignity and this colors his entire Congregation.

That said, Saint Vincent had a priestly spirituality, orienting it toward his confreres in formation, the ordinands, and the members of the Tuesday Conferences. He wanted them to be formators for the clergy.

What a great service this is, the formation of priests! New needs demand new men. The urgent need of seminaries became evident as priestly spirituality developed. Beginning in 1631, he was working for candidates for ordination, and in 1641 he opened his first seminary, at Annecy. From that point on, the formation of good priests was a major concern of his. *You will have plenty of them if you take the trouble to form them in the true spirit of their state, which consists especially in the interior life and the practice of prayer and the virtues.... What is important is to form them to solid piety and devotion.... We must be full reservoirs in order to let our water spill out without becoming empty, and we must possess the spirit with which we want them to be animated, for no one can give what he does not have.* (L 1623)

Basically, he was concerned about the salvation of everyone, and especially those left behind by the Church. The specific style of Vincentian formation is a deliberate attention to the poor. *But there's something else: the Church's need for good priests to make up for all the ignorance and vice that cover the earth and to rescue the poor Church from that deplorable state, for which good souls should weep tears of blood.* (C-CM 195)

This consideration coincides with Vincent's own spiritual journey. It knits together his kinds of activity and is a sign of his personality. It even obliges us in conscience. In the same conference he adds: *Aren't those who are poor the afflicted members of Our Lord? Aren't they our brothers and sisters? And if priests abandon them, who do you think is going to help them?*

Reflection Questions

What is my esteem for the sacrament of Holy Orders? Do I perceive the spirit of Jesus in the priests I know? What one thing could I do to help priests, especially those who are troubled and suffering?

14
Fundamental Virtues

Focus Point

////////////

Virtues are strengths of character. Vincent singled out several for his closest followers. We can meditate on our own strengths and resolve to develop others that we wish we had. To nourish us in this, we examine the virtues of Jesus.

////////////

Those then, my dear confreres, are the three Gospel teachings most in conformity with our state. The first is simplicity, which concerns God. The second is humility, which concerns our submission; by it we become a holocaust to God, to whom we owe all honor, and in whose presence we must efface ourselves and act in such a way that He may take possession of us. The third is gentleness in order to put up with our neighbor's failings. The first concerns God; the second, ourselves; and the third, our neighbor. But, the means of having these virtues is mortification, which gets rid of anything that can prevent us from acquiring them.... The fifth teaching is zeal, consisting in a pure desire to become pleasing to God and helpful to our neighbor: zeal to spread the kingdom of God and zeal to procure the salvation of our neighbor. (C-CM 211)

///////////

Saint Vincent is now pointing out the five virtues that he liked to call "fundamental," and which we can today call basic virtues: simplicity, humility, gentleness, mortification and zeal. These are the virtues proper to his Missioners. When he speaks of them, he presents them as *the faculties of the soul of the whole Congregation,* (*Vincentian Common Rules,* 2:14) and his own brand of humor compares them to *the five smooth stones … of David's sling.* (VCR 12:12) With these weapons, the Missioner can combat *mere human prudence; the desire for publicity; always wanting everyone to give in to us and see things our way; the pursuit of self-gratification in everything; attaching no great importance to either God's honor or the salvation of others.* (VCR 2:15)

Similarly, the Daughters of Charity have "three precious pearls," simplicity, humility and charity.

The appeal to virtue under all its spiritual forms was inspired by Thomas Aquinas. In addition, Vincent had read *Practice of Perfection and Christian*

Virtues by the Jesuit, Alfonso Rodriguez, a book very much in favor in the renewal of consecrated life. The author emphasized the virtues.

However, Vincent did not just stop at a static and disembodied virtue, similar to the ruminations of the classical philosophers. Rather, with the Gospels opened he loved to contemplate God, who inspires the virtuous person, or Christ, humble, gentle, simple, charitable, mortified and zealous. This is what gave him his inner energy and what concerns us today. With our gaze on God, on Jesus — this is the way of those who are called to live out a complete gift of self.

God is the author of every gift. One of these is that God orients us toward good and inspires us with a behavior worthy of Him.

The example to follow is Jesus. Vincent said that He lived according to the heart of God, which we would call living virtuously: *That He did so was apparent in the eyes of heaven and earth, and everyone who had the happiness of being with Him during His mortal life saw that He always observed the Gospel teachings. That was His goal, His glory, and His honor.* (C-CM 211) Our entire intention is to follow Jesus Christ, *to take Him as a model in the way He acted.* (C-CM 195)

Simplicity? We look toward God: *God is a simple being, who receives nothing from anyone else; He's a sovereign, infinite essence, with no admixture; He's a pure being, who never changes. Now, this virtue of the Creator is found in some creatures with whom He shares it.* (C-CM 201) He adds: *Go straight to God.* (L 1555)

What about humility? Its perspective is Christological. When we examine it, we find Christ, little, humble, rejected, who fearlessly gives himself as an example, and Vincent marvels at this: *Our Lord alone said and could say, "Learn from me, that I am gentle and humble of heart." Oh, what words! "Learn from me," not from someone else, not from a human being, but from a God; "learn from me...."* (C-CM 203) Humility imitated in this way is the humility of Jesus, which locates us in the truth of our inmost being. We are not authentic unless we are in relationship to God, who is all: *Through humility, we annihilate ourselves and establish God as the Sovereign Being.* (C-CM 211)

Why did Vincent choose meekness? Because Jesus lived it. *We should make a great effort to learn the following lesson, also taught by Jesus Christ:* "Learn from me because I am gentle and humble of heart." *We should remember that He Himself said that by gentleness we inherit the earth. If we act on this we will win people over so that they will turn to the Lord.* (VCR 2:6)

How can we live out mortification? Jesus carried his cross. There is no other way than that: *That's how we have to constantly use the knife of mortification to cut off the evil output of corrupt nature, which never tires of growing branches of its corruption so that they might prevent Jesus Christ, who is compared to the stock of the vine and who compares us to the vine shoots, from having us bear abundant fruit by the practice of the holy virtues.* (C-CM 204)

And what joy in being filled with zeal! As Vincent would say, we look to *God's pleasure,* the example of Jesus Christ: *Yes, Messieurs, we must be all for God and the service of the people; we have to give ourselves to God for that, wear ourselves out for that, and give our lives for that.* (C-CM 167) All apostolic labor is done in collaboration with Jesus Christ for the restoration of a debased creation, and its only ambition is to restore all things in Him.

Finally, how do we live out charity? It is nothing else than looking toward the Son of God, "to the heart of charity," and to follow his example of self-denial out of love for his creation: *Charity can't remain idle; it impels us to work for the salvation and consolation of others.* (C-CM 207)

These, then, are the leading virtues for those who follow Vincent. But why these and not others? The reason is that they have a specific cast to them, proper to Missioners or to the Sisters. And Vincent was right to conclude with a little smile: *Let's envelop ourselves in these five virtues like snails in their shells. Ah, these virtues we'll go everywhere with them and manage to overcome everything! Without them, we'll be Missioners in appearance only.* (C-CM 212)

Reflection Questions

What virtues or strengths of character do I perceive in myself? Where are the areas of growth and development? What are the virtues that I admire in others and would like to emulate? What is keeping me from advancing in these virtues?

15
To Serve
and Evangelize
Together

Focus Point

////////////

Whether we live alone or share our life with others, we live in community with all the faithful, joined with them in the Mystical Body of Christ. The experience of working together in a team for the kingdom of God is the theme for today's meditation.

////////////

You must also remember that your principal concern, which God asks especially of you, is to be very attentive in serving the poor, who are our lords. Oh yes, Sisters! They are our masters. That's why you must treat them gently and kindly, reflecting that this is why God has brought you together; and why He formed your Company. (C-DC 15)

//////////////

*V*incent de Paul's goal was to work together. He could not conceive of things otherwise. In fact, from the foundation of the first Confraternity of Charity in Chatillon, he began what would be called today a team. In view of the challenge posed by "Les Maladières," a hamlet outside town where an entire family was suffering, he experienced the abundance of good will in his parish but which was not organized. Just think of the waste involved! What to do about this? *Couldn't these good ladies be brought together and encouraged to give themselves to God to serve the sick poor?* (C-DC 20)

Beginning with a meeting, his organizational reflexes came to the fore, and each new "Charity" was a masterpiece of structure. The human side was clear: a rector, a prioress, the first assistant, the second assistant, the servers, etc. We sense here a practice that touched persons who were already committed, and so the regulations developed almost automatically: admission of new members, the daily schedule, charity toward the sick, visits to prisoners, spiritual assistance, and burial of the deceased poor. When these confraternities began in Paris, the members were the great ladies of the nobility, and these same women had to conform to the same rigor, despite questions of rank. Experience showed that an even greater efficacy was developing out of work done as a team and methodically. He thus responded to his initial intuition: *Because, however, it is to be feared that this good work, once begun, might die out in a short time if they do not have some union and spiritual bond among themselves to maintain it, they have arranged to form an association that can be set up as a confraternity.* (D 126)

This is a fundamental statement, and it is found in all the organizations that derive from him. The breadth and the urgency of the requests that Saint Vincent perceived oriented him always toward responses of a communitarian nature.

This was certainly true of the priests and brothers of the Congregation of the Mission. On 4 September 1626, four priests came together to form the first community. The official record stipulates that the issue was *for the maintenance of some priests who commit themselves and come together to devote themselves, by way of the mission, to catechize, preach, and exhort poor country people to make a general confession.* (D 61) They had come together for the Mission.

In the same way, the Daughters of Charity were organized in view of service, and it is interesting to see that they became, in fact, a communitarian reality.

Vincent wanted communities for evangelization or for service. We can wonder about

this purpose. An attentive rereading of Vincent
de Paul shows that community is the privileged
means to reach an effective mission. Bringing
it about implies a serious examination of conscience. When tensions, difficulties, and con-
flict arise in communities, there is that reflex
of wondering about how all these persons who
make up the community are placed in relation
to the poor.

The apostolic ministry should organize the
community in relationship to the work being
required and not the other way around. Can we
not see the importance of such an orientation
for the entire Church? Christians do not assemble for the mere pleasure of being together but
for a mission received from a superior. This
perspective engenders a new way of conceiving
community. It can make it dynamic and give it
more force and apostolic vitality.

Every legitimate mission comes from God.
This is the second element that Vincent kept in
mind. He understood that God is also the principle of community; every mandate of charity
comes from God.

The Vincentian community brings about
another dimension often pointed out by
Vincent: this is a faith reality, conceived in the
image of the Holy Trinity. This is true for both
the Missioners and for the Sisters. For example,
he pointed out: *Since God is but One in Himself,*

and in God there are three Persons, without the Father being greater than the Son or the Son being greater than the Holy Spirit, it should be the same for Daughters of Charity. They should be the image of the Most Holy Trinity; and even though they are several, they should form but one heart and one mind. (D 159)

The door is open here to fraternity.

How could one not want to enter into a relationship with the neighbor? Vincent was enthusiastic in even creating a new word to express this, mutuality. This is what he said: *O mon Dieu! yes! ... that's a real need: close communication with one another; sharing everything. Nothing is more necessary. It unites hearts, and God blesses the advice received, with the result that things go better....Nothing should happen, nothing should be done or said, unless each of you knows it. You must have this mutuality.* (D 160)

Mutuality is the result of union. Beyond simple esprit de corps, each member is united in God to his brothers or sisters. This happens in a wonderful Trinitarian fusion which gives its fullness of meaning to the Vincentian spirit. He wrote to a local superior of the Daughters of Charity: *Live together as having but one heart and one soul so that by this union of spirit you may be a true image of the unity of God, since your number represents the three Persons of the Most Holy Trinity. I pray for this to the Holy Spirit, who*

is the union of the Father and the Son, that He
may be yours likewise and give you profound peace.
(L 1389)

As we complete this meditation and this
book designed for a retreat at home, it is good
to hear Father Vincent pronounce over us
these simple but profound words that invite us
to the fulness of charity for our own good and
for that of the poor.

O Savior of our souls, by Your love You willed to
die for us, and in a certain sense departed from Your
glory to give it to us and, by this means, to make
us like gods, by making us like You yourself, as far
as that is possible. Imprint charity on our hearts so
that we may one day be able to go to join this beautiful Company of Charity that's in heaven. This
is the prayer I offer You, O Savior of our souls....
Grant then, O Lord, that they may be filled with
love of You, for their neighbor, and for one another.
(C-DC 93)

Reflection Questions

What have I become in my life? Is my way
the only way of living and working? What
have I learned from others? How have they
helped me grow? Is there any selfishness in
the ideas and opinions that I hold onto; if
so, what task lies before me? What did the
Lord show me? Was any particular spiritual

path revealed to me? Are there any particular points that I might need to return to for more reflection and prayer? What do I most want to remember? Do I feel the need to make any resolution or commitment as the result of these days of prayer?

For Further Reading

Complete Works

Coste, Pierre, *Saint Vincent de Paul correspondance, entretiens, documents,* 14 volumes, Paris, 1920–1925. English edition: *Saint Vincent de Paul. Correspondence, Conferences, Documents*; newly translated, edited, and annotated from the 1920 edition of Pierre Coste. Brooklyn, N.Y.: New City Press, 1985–2010.

Abelly, Louis, *The Life of the Venerable Servant of God Vincent de Paul: Founder and First Superior General of the Congregation of the Mission;* translated by Bro. William Quinn, edited by John E. Rybolt, 3 vols. New Rochelle, N.Y.: New City Press, 1993.

Collet, Pierre, *La Vie de saint Vincent de Paul,* 2 vols., Nancy, 1748.

Other Works

Cahiers vincentiens, thematic studies in French begun in 1972. Available from Animation vincentienne, 16, grande rue Saint-Michel, 31400 Toulouse, France.

"'On the Eminent Dignity of the Poor in the Church.' A Sermon by Jacques Bénigne Bossuet," introd. and trans. Edward R. Udovic, *Vincentian Heritage* 13:1 (1992) 37–58.

Other Studies and Biographies in English

Coste, Pierre, *The Life & Works of Saint Vincent de Paul,* translated from the French by Joseph Leonard. New Rochelle, N.Y.: New City Press, 1987.

Dodin, Andre, *Vincent de Paul and Charity: A Contemporary Portrait of His Life and Apostolic Spirit;* translated by Jean Marie Smith and Dennis Saunders; edited by Hugh O'Donnell and Marjorie Gale Hornstein. New Rochelle, N.Y.: New City Press, 1993.

Maloney, Robert P., *Go!: On the Missionary Spirituality of St. Vincent de Paul,* Salamanca, Spain (2000).

Maloney, Robert P., *He Hears the Cry of the Poor: On the Spirituality of Vincent de Paul,* Hyde Park, N.Y.: New City Press, 1995.

Maloney, Robert P., *Seasons in Spirituality: Reflections on Vincentian Spirituality in Today's World.* Hyde Park, N.Y.: New City Press, 1998.

Mezzadri, Luigi, *A Short Life of Saint Vincent de Paul*, translated by Thomas Davitt. Dublin, Ireland, 1992.

Mezzadri, Luigi, and Román, José-María, *The Vincentians. A General History of the Congregation of the Mission,* vol. 1, Hyde Park, N.Y.: New City Press, 2009.

Pujo, Bernard, *Vincent de Paul, The Trailblazer,* translated by Gertrud Graubart Champe, Notre Dame, Ind., 2003.

Note: Many of the titles in the bibliography are available electronically: http://via.library.depaul.edu/vdp/.

Saint Francis of Assisi *(Thadée Matura, O.F.M.)*
978-1-56548-315-6, paper

Saint Francis de Sales *(Claude Morel)*
978-0764-805752, paper

Henri Nouwen *(Robert Waldron)*
978-1-56548-324-8, paper

Saint Jean Jugan *(Michel Lafon)*
978-1-56548-329-3, paper

Saint John of the Cross *(Constant Tonnelier)*
978-0764-806544, paper

Saint Katharine Drexel *(Leo Luke Marcello)*
978-0764-809231, paper

Saint Louis de Montfort *(Veronica Pinardon)*
978-0764-807152, paper

Saint Martín de Porres: A Saint of the Americas *(Brian J. Pierce)*
978-0764-812163, paper

Meister Eckhart *(André Gozier)*
978-0764-806520, paper

Thomas Merton *(André Gozier)*
978-1-56548-330-9, paper

Saint Elizabeth Ann Seton *(Betty Ann McNeil)*
978-0764-808418, paper

Johannes Tauler *(André Pinet)*
978-0764-806537, paper

Saint Teresa of Ávila *(Jean Abiven)*
978-0764-805738, paper

Saint Thomas Aquinas *(André Pinet)*
978-0764-806568, paper

NEW CITY PRESS
www.newcitypress.com
1-800-462-5980

**Thank you for choosing this book.
If you would like to receive regular information
about New City Press titles, please fill in this card.**

Title purchased:—————————————————————

Please check the subjects that are of particular interest to you:

- ○ **FATHERS OF THE CHURCH**
- ○ **CLASSICS IN SPIRITUALITY**
- ○ **CONTEMPORARY SPIRITUALITY**
- ○ **THEOLOGY**
- ○ **SCRIPTURE AND COMMENTARIES**
- ○ **FAMILY LIFE**
- ○ **BIOGRAPHY / HISTORY**
- ○ **INSPIRATION / GIFT**

Other subjects of interest: —————————————————

(please print)

Name: —————————————————————————————

Address: ————————————————————————————

——————————————————————————————————

Telephone: ————————————————————————————

NEW CITY PRESS
202 CARDINAL RD.
HYDE PARK, NY 12538

Place
Stamp
Here